Acknowledgements

CW00384579

My thanks still go to my boyfriend, Matthe
throughout the writing process and helped me understand the Wall Street
Crash.

Thanks to Liss, who pointed out that Steinbeck couldn't truly understand the
working man.

Thanks, as ever, to Freja for her editing skills.

Thanks to everyone who has bought my books so far, now across at least two
countries.

Many thanks to my family, both biological and extended, who have been
impressed and pleasantly surprised that I can write.

About the Author

Katherine holds a BA and MA in History, a PGCE in English and a 100 metre
swimming certificate. She worked in schools in South London for five years,
ran a school in China and now works with students who are withdrawn from
mainstream education. In her spare time she runs the Straight Talking
English podcast, tweets a lot, goes to vintage shops, eats Italian food and
plans extravagant holidays she can't really afford.

straighttalkingenglish.com

New podcast episodes weekly on Spotify, Soundcloud, iTunes, Stitcher and
Castbox.

@str8talkenglish on Twitter

Content Warning

Featured in this book are references which some readers may find upsetting. These include:

- Intimate partner violence in 'A Woman's Place'.
- Racial slurs and discussions of racially-motivated violence in 'Race and Identity' and 'The American Dream'.
- Use of the term 'gypsy' in 'Something That Happened'.
- Animal cruelty in 'Violence and the Landscape'.

The references are in addition to potentially upsetting language included in Of Mice and Men, such as Candy's repeated slurs towards Crooks, descriptions of animal cruelty and two murders.

The language used in this book does not reflect the views of the author and it is included to give a full picture of the context which inspired this novella.

The American Dream and the Roaring Twenties

For those of you who think Steinbeck's account of life on the farm in the 1930s is not relevant to today, think again. One of the main issues necessary to consider when engaging with this novella was one of the hot-button issues of Donald Trump's 2016 election campaign, and has continued to be so for the last three years (at the time of writing).

"'Sadly, the American dream is dead," Donald Trump proclaimed when he announced his candidacy for president of the United States.' [1]

Vice President Mike Pence jumped into the debate and informed commentators that reports of the American Dream's death had been premature.

'Was the American dream in trouble? You bet. I really do believe that's why the American people chose a president whose family lived the American dream and was willing to go in and fight to make the American dream available for every American.' [2]

However, in February 2019, political scientist Samuel J Abrams gleefully reported that:

---

[1] Sarah Churchwell, *'End of the American dream? The dark history of 'America first'*, accessed 11/19. https://www.theguardian.com/books/2018/apr/21/end-of-the-american-dream-the-dark-history-of-america-first

[2] Ashley Turner, *'Mike Pence says the American dream was 'dying' before Trump became president'*, accessed 11/19. https://www.cnbc.com/2019/04/11/mike-pence-says-the-american-dream-was-dying-until-trump-was-inaugurated.html

'I am pleased to report that the American dream is alive and well for an overwhelming majority of Americans.' [3]

This is a novella about the American Dream and a conflict between American Dreams. The definition of this concept is just as vague now as it was in the 1930s, and while it's difficult to define, it's easier to see how different characters took different American Dreams and turned them into the sources of disagreement throughout Of Mice and Men.

As soon as America became a separate nation in 1776, the idea that a person can follow their own quest for happiness became a priority. This was even enshrined in the Declaration of Independence in an iconic line.

'We hold these truths to be self-evident, that all men are created equal, that they are endowed by their Creator with certain unalienable Rights, that among these are Life, Liberty and the pursuit of Happiness.' [4]

However, this pursuit of happiness became really ill defined. The American Dream became a concept which defined an American Identity, but it was never really made clear what it was. It's easier to address Of Mice and Men as a novel of the death of the American Dream if we take each character who engages with it separately, since every character with a dream is associated with a different shard of the Dream.

Despite working towards the ranch, George holds a secret dream.

---

[3] Samuel J Abrams, *'The American Dream is Alive and Well'*, accessed 10/19. https://www.nytimes.com/2019/02/05/opinion/american-dream.html?module=inline

[4] Various, *'The Declaration of Independence'*, accessed 10/19. https://www.archives.gov/founding-docs/declaration-transcript

'God a'mighty, if I was alone I could live so easy. I could go get a job an' work, an' no trouble. No mess at all, and when the end of the month come I could take my fifty bucks[5] and go into town and get whatever I want. Why, I could stay in a cat house all night. I could eat any place I want, hotel or any place, and order any damn thing I could think of. An' I could do all that every damn month. Get a gallon of whisky, or set in a pool room and play cards or shoot pool.'[6]

This dream can be summarised as a dream of consumption, of being able to access all the pleasures of the 1920s. This was the boom decade of new products and free time earned by no longer doing everything by hand. This desire to access these commodities was inflamed by the use of what can be considered modern advertising.

'Mass advertising campaigns were launched to encourage consumers to buy, use and buy again. . . The goal of advertising, said Bruce Barton [founding member of a famous advertising firm] is to arouse desires and stimulate wants, to make people dissatisfied with the old and out of date and by constant iteration to send them to work harder to get the latest model— whether that model be an icebox or a rug or a new home.

While advertising fanned the flame of desire for new goods, new forms of credit—noticeably instalment buying—enabled consumers to buy them. 'Ride Now, Pay Later' trumpeted auto manufacturers. Advertising raised expectations and fostered a belief in Americans that they were entitled to an ever-rising standard of living. In the past, most people had thought it immoral to go into debt. Now, they were inspired by advertising to seek instant

---

[5] $871 in 1937, £668 at time of writing.

[6] Steinbeck, John (2006 ed), *Of Mice and Men,* UK: Penguin, 12.

gratification. Old-fashioned notions of thrift and self-restraint were replaced by the urge to consume.' [7]

However, George is a rural farmworker. For him, the 1920s would have not been a decade of increased leisure time and a higher standard of living. For a start, his wages would probably have gone down.

'The average wage of the farmworker, which had climbed to $830[8] in 1920, slipped back to $551[9] in 1924.' [10]

Economically, George has little chance of achieving this, especially with Lennie around. Logistically he also has little chance of achieving this since just going to a bar would be a nightmare trip.

'In 1914 there were only 750 miles of concrete highway in the entire country. Most roads were merely dirt or gravel tracks, and were often washed out or quagmires. Maps of rural America were also non-existent as was information on road conditions.' [11]

Even the simple dream at the opening of the novella is never going to happen.

Curley's wife, however, dreams of fame and fortune.

---

[7] Miller, Nathan (2003), New World Coming: The 1920s and the Making of Modern America, US: Da Capo Press, 151.

[8] $10,420.93 in 2018, or £8,041.52 at time of writing.

[9] $8,091.22 in 2018 or £6243.74 at time of writing. A car would cost $525 in the early 1920s, a two course lunch might be 16c and rent might be $15/month.

[10] Miller, New World Coming, 150.

[11] Miller, New World Coming, 190.

'Coulda been in the movies, an' had nice clothes—all them nice clothes like they wear. An' I coulda sat in them big hotels, an' had pitchers took of me. When they had them previews I coulda went to them, an' spoke in the radio, an' it wouldn'ta cost me a cent because I was in the pitcher. An' all them nice clothes like they wear. Because this guy says I was a natural.' [12]

This was a very common dream in the 1920s, as it still is today. This decade saw the birth of Hollywood as we know it, and the demand for movies was huge.

'By the mid-1920s movie theaters were selling 50 million tickets each week, a sum equal to roughly half the US population!' [13]

Is Curley's wife's dream likely to have come true? In a word, no. It's another example of an empty pipe dream. Just a quick glance at the ways other successful actresses had their big breaks will tell anyone that being a farmer's wife who grew up in the middle of nowhere in California was not the way to go about it. Take Mary Pickford's entry into Hollywood:

'When Pickford was five and still named Gladys Smith, her widowed mother Charlotte allowed a travelling theatre couple to put her on stage for a fee. The applause was great; the cash was better. Pickford was driven by success, almost frighteningly so, even in her first years as an actress. She'd stab her cheeks with a hair pin to imitate the older blushing beauties. School was out —Pickford only attended for three months—and instead learned how to read from the billboards she'd spot on the road. (She claimed a lifelong hatred of cerise, the dark-red colour of train seats.)

---

[12] Steinbeck, *Of Mice and Men*, 100.

[13] Zeitz, *'Age of Convergence'*.

She'd met deMille when she performed in his play on Broadway at the age of 15. His younger brother Cecil (who capitalised the family name to make it 'DeMille') was another cast member. Both men would become big names in Hollywood—years after Pickford showed the doubters that it could be done. She arrived in 1910, the month before Hollywood even got its official name, as the rising star of DW Griffith's Biograph Company.' [14]

Bebe Daniels has a different, but still more conventional, start to a Hollywood career.

'She came from a show business family with an actress mother and a theater manager father and she first appeared on stage at the age of 4. She started her film career aged 8 and worked for a number of studios, including Imperial, and Pathe and she was the first screen Dorothy in 1910 in 'The Wonderful Wizard of Oz'.

When she was just 14 she was chosen to join Hal Roach's comedy studio as Harold Lloyd's co-star in a long series of "Lonesome Luke" two-reel shorts starting with 'Giving Them Fits' in 1915.

After four years and a highly publicised romance with Harold Lloyd Bebe decided her career needed greater variety and she signed a contract with producer/director Cecil B. Demille, appearing in a number of silent movies, usually in glamorous, non-starring roles, over the next two years.' [15]

The hope of being 'discovered' at a rural party just seems to make the reader feel more sympathy for Curley's wife. It will never happen.

---

[14] Amy Nicholson, *'Mary Pickford: The Woman Who Shaped Hollywood'*, accessed 11/19. http://www.bbc.com/culture/story/20190204-mary-pickford-the-woman-who-shaped-hollywood

[15] Chris Whitely, *'Bebe Daniels'*, accessed 11/19. http://www.hollywoodsgoldenage.com/actors/bebe_daniels.html

On the face of it, George and Lennie's dream seems the most typical of any American Dream held by any character.

‘Lennie pleaded, "Come on, George. Tell me. Please, George. Like you done before."

"You get a kick outa that, don't you? Awright, I'll tell you, and then we'll eat our supper...."

George's voice became deeper. He repeated his words rhythmically as though he had said them many times before. "Guys like us, that work on ranches, are the loneliest guys in the world. They got no fambly. They don't belong no place. They come to a ranch an' work up a stake and then they go into town and blow their stake, and the first thing you know they're poundin' their tail on some other ranch. They ain't got nothing to look ahead to."

Lennie was delighted. "That's it- that's it. Now tell how it is with us."

George went on. "With us it ain't like that. We got a future. We got somebody to talk to that gives a damn about us. We don't have to sit in no bar room blowin' in our jack jus' because we got no place else to go. If them other guys gets in jail they can rot for all anybody gives a damn. But not us."

Lennie broke in. "But not us! An' why? Because... because I got you to look after me, and you got me to look after you, and that's why." He laughed delightedly. "Go on now, George!"

"You got it by heart. You can do it yourself."

"No, you. I forget some a' the things. Tell about how it's gonna be."

"O.K. Someday- we're gonna get the jack together and we're gonna have a little house and a couple of acres an' a cow and some pigs and-"

"An' live off the fatta the lan'," Lennie shouted. "An' have rabbits. Go on, George! Tell about what we're gonna have in the garden and about the rabbits in the cages and about the rain in the winter and the stove, and how thick the cream is on the milk like you can hardly cut it. Tell about that, George."

"Why'n't you do it yourself? You know all of it."

"No... you tell it. It ain't the same if I tell it. Go on... George. How I get to tend the rabbits."

"Well," said George, "we'll have a big vegetable patch and a
rabbit hutch and chickens. And when it rains in the winter, we'll just say the hell with goin' to work, and we'll build up a fire in the stove and set around it an' listen to the rain comin' down on the roof- Nuts!" He took out his pocket knife. "I ain't got time for no more."' [16]

This was a dream that had been pitched at Americans for a long time, and examples go back as far as the founding of the Old West, where pioneers were encouraged to buy land in the middle of nowhere in the hope it would become better later.

'Why, this wasteland could be England or Missouri, if plowed in the right way. Brochures were distributed in Europe, the American South, and at major ports of entry to the US: "500,000 acres offered for sale as farm homes" and cheap as well, the land selling for $13 an acre. Twice a month, agents for the syndicate[17] rounded up five hundred people and put them on a train from Kansas City to the Texas Panhandle to see for themselves. The train ride was free.

Speculators who bought from the syndicate turned around and added to the claims. "Riches in the soil, prosperity in the air, progress everywhere, an Empire in the making!"

. . .Well sure, it rained less than twenty inches a year, which was the accepted threshold for growing a crop without irrigation, but through the

---

[16] Steinbeck, *Of Mice and Men,* 15.

[17] Estate agents.

miracle of dry farming a fellow could turn this land into gold. Put a windmill in
and up comes water for your hogs, chickens, and garden. And dryland wheat,
it didn't need irrigation. Just plant in the fall, when a little moisture would
bring the sprouts up, let it go dormant in the winter, then wait for spring rains
to get the crop growing again. Harvest in summer. Any three-toed fool could
do it, the agents said.' [18]

These claims were what partially led to the hideous Dust Bowl of the 1930s.
George and Lennie's dream is a nostalgic recycling of a very old myth.
Would Crooks be able to share any of the American Dreams held by the other
characters? Perhaps, but it's reasonable to assume that his would hold a
slightly different focus. From the second he is mentioned in the novella, he is
marked as different from the others using racially offensive language.

'George lifted his tick and looked underneath it. He leaned over
and inspected the sacking closely. Immediately Lennie got up and did the
same with his bed. Finally George seemed satisfied. He unrolled his bindle
and put things on the shelf, his razor and bar of soap, his comb and bottle of
pills, his liniment and leather wristband. Then he made his bed up neatly with
blankets. The old man said, "I guess the boss'll be out here in a minute. He
was sure burned when you wasn't here this morning. Come right in when we
was eatin' breakfast and says, 'Where the hell's them new men?' An' he give
the stable buck hell, too."

George patted a wrinkle out of his bed, and sat down. "Give the stable buck
hell?" he asked.

"Sure. Ya see the stable buck's a nigger."

---

[18] Egan, *The Worst Hard Time*, 24.

"Nigger, huh?"

"Yeah. Nice fella too. Got a crooked back where a horse kicked him. The boss gives him hell when he's mad. But the stable buck don't give a damn about that. He reads a lot. Got books in his room."

"What kind of a guy is the boss?" George asked.

"Well, he's a pretty nice fella. Gets pretty mad sometimes, but he's pretty nice. Tell ya what- know what he done Christmas? Brang a gallon of whisky right in here and says, 'Drink hearty, boys. Christmas comes but once a year.'"

"The hell he did! Whole gallon?"

"Yes sir. Jesus, we had fun. They let the nigger come in that night. Little skinner name of Smitty took after the nigger. Done pretty good, too. The guys wouldn't let him use his feet, so the nigger got him. If he coulda used his feet, Smitty says he woulda killed the nigger.

The guys said on account of the nigger's got a crooked back, Smitty can't use his feet." He paused in relish of the memory. "After that the guys went into Soledad and raised hell. I didn't go in there. I ain't got the poop no more.'" [19]

Crooks lived at a time when the Jim Crow laws prevented him from having the full rights due to him as an American Citizen based on his race. He also lived at a time of segregation, which explains why he can't live in the

---

[19] Steinbeck, *Of Mice and Men*, 22.

13

bunkhouse with the other men. In 1926, a good eleven years before Of Mice and Men, President Harding had made his views on race relations very clear:

'I believe the federal government should stamp out lynching[20] and remove that stain from the fair name of America . . .I believe Negro citizens of America should be guaranteed the enjoyment of all their rights . . .they have earned the full measure of citizenship bestowed.' [21]

Crooks has been promised an improvement in his situation that had not materialised, and this improvement in his rights is exactly what his participation in George and Lennie's dream will entail. This dream is also shattered by the end of the novella.

Candy, the elderly swamper[22], buys into George and Lennie's dream too, hoping in exchange for his compensation check (given after a farming accident led to the loss of a hand) he will get to live out his retirement in peace and safety. Considering that life is fair rotten for all the ranch hands, Candy's life is not the worst. He does have a limited safety net.

'The defining event of the 1930s the Great Depression, brought a resurgence in the Eugenics[23] Movement. This time eugenicists based their arguments on economics instead of genetics. These arguments, and the notion of Darwin's

---

[20] The crime of publicly murdering someone seen to be breaking a rule in a community. In this context, 'Lynching' usually refers to a group of white people deciding to murder a black person because they disliked something they did. A famous example is Emmett Till, a young black man who was publicly hanged for allegedly whistling at a white woman. These crimes had virtually no repercussions for the murderers.

[21] Churchwell, Sarah (2018), *Behold America: A History of America First and The American Dream*, UK: Bloomsbury, 134.

[22] Cleaner.

[23] The pseudo-science of improving a human population by controlled breeding to increase the occurrence of desirable heritable characteristics.

'survival of the fittest', proved persuasive as competition for a scarce number of jobs became brutal.

Paradoxically, the decade saw the election of FDR, the first president with a physical impairment. Using a wheelchair for mobility due to polio, Roosevelt's disability was not widely known by the public. During most of Roosevelt's public appearances he was not seen in his wheelchair and was often placed at the podium to appear as if he was standing on his own.

Although he downplayed his own disability, Roosevelt brought the concept of social security to America through his New Deal. As part of the Social Security Act, public assistance was extended to 'the blind and children with disabilities'. Ironically, his belief in a social safety-net for citizens with disabilities contrasted the fact that the work relief programs his administration devised often discriminated against individuals with disabilities.' [24]

This sounds promising, but the reality of this new social security was awful, as Victoria Brignell explains:

'For much of the 20th century, it was common in the UK and USA to segregate disabled people from the rest of society.

Large numbers of British and American disabled people were put away in institutions on the grounds that it was for their own good and the good of society. For example, in 1913, the passing of the Mental Incapacity Act in Britain led to around 40,000 men and women being locked away, having been deemed "feeble-minded" or "morally defective". Many disabled people living in hospitals, special schools and care homes are known to have suffered severe emotional and physical abuse.

---

[24] LEAP, *'History of Disability Rights'*, accessed 11/19. https://www.leapinfo.org/advocacy/history-of-disability-rights/1930s

Institutions regularly regarded their disabled residents as second-class citizens and showed them little respect. Staff often made little attempt to empathise with disabled people's experiences, denying them autonomy, choice and dignity and at times deliberately causing them pain and discomfort. In care homes and special schools for disabled children, there was sometimes hardly any attempt to meet the children's emotional needs or acknowledge their individual identities.

In Pride against Prejudice by Jenny Morris, one disabled woman recounts her childhood experiences of living in various institutions in England in the 1940s and 1950s. In one place, disabled children had to go outdoors at 6am every morning and weren't allowed to put bedclothes over themselves at night. For half the day they were not permitted to speak so they spent much of their time making paper darts and trying to throw messages to each other. Children never had their own toys and when they were sick they were expected to eat their own vomit. When the girl's father gave her a doll for her 11th birthday, the staff wouldn't allow her to keep it.

If the nurses took a dislike to a child they would hold her under the water in a bath until she started to go blue. A group of children would be assembled to watch what was happening. On one occasion, the nurses held a child under the water for too long and the child drowned. It was impossible for the children to tell the outside world about what went on inside the institution. All letters written by the children to their parents were censored and staff were always present when the children had visitors.' [25]

---

[25] Victoria Brignell, *'When the Disabled were Segregated'*, accessed 11/19. https://www.newstatesman.com/society/2010/12/disabled-children-british

Candy's involvement in the Dream is therefore not a vision of relaxation, but also of survival, since an elderly disabled man may well have ended up in an institution that was the stuff of nightmares.

To say Of Mice and Men is a novel of the American Dream is very true, but Steinbeck is also acknowledging the multiple American Dreams that his peers believed in, and how, in fact, most of them were futile.

The Great Depression

'Sure, I remember the Nineteen Thirties, the terrible, troubled, triumphant, surging Thirties. I can't think of any decade in history where so much happened in so many directions. Violent changes took place. Our country was modelled, our lives remoulded, our Government rebuilt, forced to functions, duties and responsibilities it had never before and can never relinquish.' [26]

This was how Steinbeck chose to introduce the decade of his most productive writing to his journalistic audience. He was somewhat underplaying the crisis which faced many of the American people, but to explain this crisis and the effects that it had, we need to step back in time to the 1920s.

In 1929 the financier John J Raskob wrote an article offering financial tips to the Ladies Home Journal. The advice he gave was slightly different to what might have been expected.

'Suppose a man marries at the age of twenty-three and begins a regular saving of fifteen dollars a month—and almost anyone who is employed can do that if he tries. If he invests in good common stocks and allows the dividends and rights to accumulate, he will at the end of twenty years have at least eighty thousand dollars and an income from investments of around four hundred dollars a month. He will be rich. And because anyone can do that I am firm in my belief that anyone not only can be rich but ought to be rich.' [27]

---

[26] Steinbeck, *America*, 17.

[27] John J Raskob, *'Everybody Ought To Be Rich'*, accessed 11/19. https://www.joshuakennon.com/wp-content/uploads/2013/01/Everybody-Ought-to-Be-Rich.pdf

One way people were encouraged to make money was to invest in stocks and shares.

'They were, most of them, amateurs, fair game for the insiders. They bought stock, most of it on margin (10 percent down and learn to pray) through so many bankers' loans that by September 1929 the total amount loaned out by brokers had skittered up from $3.2 billion to $8.5 billion (by comparison the entire federal budget for that year was only $3.1 billion). On their lunch hours, they crowded into the customer's rooms of the brokerage houses, feverish young men and heated elders, eyes intent upon the ticker tape.[28] *Twenty percent of them, it was estimated, were women; these sat with other women put aside for their use, as if the excitement go watching the ticker tape could explode into sexual frenzy if the sexes were allowed to sit together.'* [29]

William Benton, a former advertising executive, remembers this time fondly:

'In 1929, most of your Wall Street manipulators called it The New Era. They felt it was the start of a perpetual boom that would carry us on and on into new pastures' [30]

Steinbeck also remembered the optimism of this time well.

'We had it made (I didn't but most people did). I remember the drugged and happy faces of people who built paper fortunes on stocks they couldn't possibly have paid for. "I made ten grand in ten minutes today. Let's see— that's eighty thousand for the week".

---

[28] The reports on how the value of their shares were rising and falling.

[29] Watkins, *The Great Depression*, 39.

[30] Quoted in Terkel, *Hard Times*, 61.

In our little town bank presidents and track workers rushed to pay phones too call brokers[31]. Everyone was a broker, more or less. At lunch hour, store clerks and stenographers[32] munched sandwiches while they watched the stock boards and calculated their pyramiding fortunes. Their eyes had the look you see around the roulette table.

I saw it sharply because I was on the outside, writing books no-one would buy. I didn't have even the margin to start my fortune. I saw the wild spending, the champagne and caviar through the windows, smelled the heady perfumes on fur-draped ladies when they came warm and shining out the theatres.'[33]

With so much demand for shares, the prices of them naturally rose, and kept rising. Despite being advertised as this being a permanent situation, some people realised it would not be and began to 'cash out' their shares. One of these was the industrialist, Arthur Robertson:

'I recognised [the Crash] was coming in May and saved myself a lot of money. I sold a good deal of my stocks in May. It was a case of becoming frightened.'[34]

By 24th October there were overwhelming numbers of these 'sell orders' coming in to Wall Street, which sent the values of stock still held tumbling and wiped out the value of many companies. These companies had to close, causing massive unemployment. Of course, it was not only the collapse of

---

[31] A broker is the intermediary who buys and sells stocks to the average person.

[32] Typists.

[33] Steinbeck, *America and Americans*, 18.

[34] Quoted in Terkel, *Hard Times*, 68.

the stock market which caused an economic depression. After the First World War the USA's economy became increasingly linked with those of European countries who had to deal with their own problems like reconstruction after the War and hyperinflation.

Mainstream stock ownership was not the cause of many people's hardship during the 1930s. In fact, only a minority even fell for the idea of buying stock on speculation.

'Most Americans did not own stock: at no time did more than 1.5 million people purchase shares of the stock market. At the most, 4 million people owned some stock—through gifts, inheritance or purchase—in a nation of 120 million. What Americans still did was work the land. In 1929, the jobs of nearly one in four people were on a farm. The country had one foot in the fields, one foot in a bathtub of gin in the city.' [35]

Some of that proportion of Americans were, of course, the subjects of Of Mice and Men. Life had been awful for farmers for a long time since America had been in the grip of an agricultural depression for almost the entirety of the 1920s.

'The onset of World War I in 1914 sparked an economic boom for farmers in the United States. Demand for agricultural products soared as the war-ravaged countries of Europe could no longer produce needed supplies. This created a shortage that drove up prices for farm commodities. In Minnesota, the season-average price per bushel of corn rose from fifty-nine cents in 1914 to $1.30 in 1919. Wheat prices jumped from $1.05 per bushel to $2.34. The average price of hogs increased from $7.40 to $16.70 per hundred pounds, and the price of milk rose from $1.50 to $2.95 per hundred pounds.

[35] Egan, Timothy (2006), *The Worst Hard Time: The Untold Story of Those Who Survived The Great American Dustbowl*, New York: Houghton Mifflin Harcourt, 74.

To meet the demand, the US government encouraged farmers to produce more. In 1916, Congress passed the Federal Farm Loan Act, creating twelve federal land banks to provide long-term loans for farm expansion. Believing that the boom would continue, many farmers took advantage of this and other loan opportunities to invest in land, tractors, and other new labor-saving equipment at interest rates ranging from 5 to 7 percent. By 1920, 52.4 percent of the 132,744 Minnesota farms reporting to the Agricultural Census carried mortgage debt, totaling more than $254 million.

After the US entered the war in 1917 and continuing into the post-war years, 40 million acres of uncultivated land in the US went under the plow, including 30 million acres in the wheat- and corn-producing states of the Midwest. In Kittson County alone, wheat acreage increased from 93,000 acres prewar to 146,000 acres. Minnesota farmers had nearly 18.5 million acres under cultivation by 1929. The demand for land inflated the price of farm real estate, regardless of quality. The average price of Minnesota farm land more than doubled between 1910 and 1920, from $46 to $109 per acre.

After the end of the war, relief efforts kept the demand for US agricultural products high. Gross exports of all grains in 1918–1919 totaled 525,461,560 bushels. During that period, the US shipped more than 2.9 billion pounds of pork, 1.1 billion pounds of beef, and nearly 8.8 million pounds of dairy products to allied countries, various relief programs, and American Expeditionary Forces overseas.

Farmers continued to produce more, expecting demand and prices to remain stable. As Europe began to recover from the war, however, the US farm economy began a long downward trend that reached a crisis during the Great Depression. Minnesota farmers' gross cash income fell from $438 million in 1918 to $229 million in 1922. In 1932, it fell to $155 million.

With heavy debts to pay and improved farming practices and equipment making it easier to work more land, farmers found it hard to reduce production. The resulting large surpluses caused farm prices to plummet. From 1919 to 1920, corn tumbled from $1.30 per bushel to forty-seven cents, a drop of more than 63 percent. Wheat prices fell to $1.65 per bushel. The price of hogs dropped to $12.90 per hundred pounds.

As surpluses mounted, the federal government promoted lowering production. It also created programs designed to help stabilize prices. The goal was to achieve parity—to bring prices back to prewar levels and equalize the prices farmers received with the prices they paid for goods.

Foreign trade restrictions, such as the Fordney–McCumber Tariff (1922) and the Hawley-Smoot Tariff (1930), imposed high taxes on imports in an attempt to protect US farms and industry. International trading partners reacted by increasing import fees on American goods. US export of farm products declined, surpluses grew, and prices continued to drop. In 1932, Minnesota corn prices fell to twenty-eight cents per bushel, wheat dropped to forty-four cents per bushel, and the price of hogs fell 75 percent to $3.20 per hundred pounds.

With less demand for land, real estate values plunged to an average of $35 per acre by the late 1930s. Farmers struggled to repay loans for land that had lost its value. Rising property taxes, freight rates, and labor costs added to the financial hardships facing many farmers. In Minnesota, the average tax per acre increased from forty-six cents in 1913 to $1.45 in 1930.' [36]

[36] Linda Cameron, *'Agricultural Depression, 1920–1934'*, accessed 11/19. https://www.mnopedia.org/agricultural-depression-1920-1934

This meant, in real terms, people were losing their homes when they could not meet their mortgage and credit card payments.

'By 1932, a third of all farmers on the plains faced foreclosure for back taxes or debts: nationwide, one in twenty were losing their land. And since more Americans worked on a farm than any other places, it meant every state was swimming in the same drowning pool.' [37]

Just to make everything worse, in addition to being forced to pay back loans on the spot, the banks where the money was held closed. Today we have laws in place to protect consumers' money should a bank cease to operate, but in the 1930s a local independent bank would be the literal holder of your money in a vault. If the bank closed, your money was gone forever. Many banks had caught on to investment fever, or lent strongly to companies which closed, leading them to be a much victims of the Crash as individual investors. It was also a knock-on effect that caused huge amounts of harm to those who were never even involved with business or the Stock Market. With no money and no way of earning money, people began to starve and grow desperate.

Virginia Durr, who later became a civil rights activist, reflected on this era.

'It was a time of terrible suffering. The contradictions were so obvious that it didn't take a very bright person to realize something was terribly wrong. Have you ever seen a child with rickets? Shaking as with palsy. No proteins, no milk. And the companies pouring milk into gutters. People with nothing to wear, and they were plowing up cotton. People with nothing to eat, and they killed the pigs. If that wasn't the craziest system in the world, could you imagine anything more idiotic? This was just insane.

---

[37] Egan, *The Worst Hard Time*, 104.

And people blamed themselves, not the system. They felt they had been at fault: . . . "if we hadn't bought that old radio" . . ."if we hadn't bought that old secondhand car." Among the things that horrified me were the preachers— the fundamentalists. They would tell the people they suffered because of their sins. And the people believed it. God was punishing them. Their children were starving because of their sins.

People who were independent, who thought they were masters and mistresses of their lives, were all of a sudden dependent on others. Relatives or relief. People of pride went into shock and sanitoriums. My mother was one.

Up to this time, I had been a conformist, a Southern snob. I actually thought the only people who amounted to anything were the very small group which I belonged to. The fact that my family wasn't as well off as those of the girls I went with—I was vice president of the Junior League—made me value even more the idea of being well-born . . . .

What I learned during the Depression changed all that. I saw a blinding light like Saul on the road to Damascus. (Laughs.) It was the first time I had seen the other side of the tracks. The rickets, the pellagra—it shook me up. I saw the world as it really was . . . .

The Depression affected people in two different ways. The great majority reacted by thinking money is the most important thing in the world. Get yours. And get it for your children. Nothing else matters. Not having that stark terror come at you again . . . .

And then there was a small number of people who felt the whole system was lousy. You have to change it. The kids come along and they want to change

25

it, too. But they don't seem to know what to put in its place. I'm not so sure I know, either. I do think it has to be responsive to people's needs. And it has to be done by democratic means, if possible.' [38]

Elizabeth Barth, a former charity worker, remembers the psychological effects of the poverty she saw.

'I'll never forget one of the first families I visited. The father was a railroad man who had lost his job. I was told by my supervisor that I really had to see the poverty. If a family needed clothing, I was to investigate how much clothing they had at hand. So I looked into this man's closet—[pauses, it becomes difficult]—he was a tall, gray-haired man, though not terribly old. He let me look in his closet—he was so insulted. [She weeps angrily.] He said, "Why are you doing this?" I remember his feeling of humiliation . . . the terrible humiliation. [She can't continue. After a pause, she resumes.] He said, "I really haven't anything to hide, but if you really must look into it. . . ." I could see he was very proud. He was so deeply humiliated. And I was, too. . . ."' [39]

Emma Tiller and her husband were farmers when the Great Depression began in 1929.

'This horrible way of liven' with almost nothin' lasted up until Roosevelt. There was another strangest thing. I didn't suffer for food through the Thirties, because there was plenty of people that really suffered much worse. When you go through a lot, you in better condition to survive through all these kinds of things.

---

[38] Studs Terkel, *'Firsthand Accounts of the Great Depression'*, accessed 11/19. https://www.facinghistory.org/mockingbird/firsthand-accounts-great-depression

[39] Terkel, *'Firsthand accounts'*.

I picked cotton. We weren't getting but thirty-five cents a hundred, but I was able to make it. 'Cause I also worked people's homes, where they give you old clothes and shoes.

At this time, I worked in private homes a lot and when the white people kill hogs, they always get the Negroes to help. The cleanin' of the insides and the clean up the mess afterwards. And then they would give you a lot of scraps. A pretty adequate amount of meat for the whole family. The majority of the Negroes on the farm were in the same shape we were in. The crops were eaten by these worms. And they had no other jobs except farming.

In 1934, in this Texas town, the farmers was all out of food. The government gave us a slip, where you could pick up food. For a week, they had people who would come and stand in line, and they couldn't get waited on. This was a small town, mostly white. Only five of us in that line were Negroes, the rest was white. We would stand all day and wait and wait and wait. And get nothin' or if you did, it was spoiled meat. . . .

The Government sent two men out there to find out why the trouble. They found out his man and a couple others had rented a huge warehouse and was stackin' that food and sellin' it. The food that was supposed to be issued to these people. These three men was sent to the pen.' [40]

The 'Roosevelt' who Emma mentions is Franklin Delano Roosevelt, credited with solving a great deal of the economic problems facing America with a series of policies called the New Deal.

---

[40] Terkel, *'Firsthand accounts'.*

'On March 4, 1933, during the bleakest days of the Great Depression, newly elected President Franklin D. Roosevelt delivered his first inaugural address before 100,000 people on Washington's Capitol Plaza.

"First of all," he said, "let me assert my firm belief that the only thing we have to fear is fear itself."

He promised that he would act swiftly to face the "dark realities of the moment" and assured Americans that he would "wage a war against the emergency" just as though "we were in fact invaded by a foreign foe." His speech gave many people confidence that they'd elected a man who was not afraid to take bold steps to solve the nation's problems.

The next day, Roosevelt declared a four-day bank holiday to stop people from withdrawing their money from shaky banks. On March 9, Congress passed Roosevelt's Emergency Banking Act, which reorganized the banks and closed the ones that were insolvent.

In his first "fireside chat" three days later, the president urged Americans to put their savings back in the banks, and by the end of the month almost three quarters of them had reopened.

Roosevelt's quest to end the Great Depression was just beginning. Next, he asked Congress to take the first step toward ending Prohibition—one of the more divisive issues of the 1920s—by making it legal once again for Americans to buy beer. (At the end of the year, Congress ratified the 21st Amendment and ended Prohibition for good.)

In May, he signed the Tennessee Valley Authority Act into law, creating the TVA and enabling the federal government to build dams along the

Tennessee River that controlled flooding and generated inexpensive hydroelectric power for the people in the region.

That same month, Congress passed a bill that paid commodity farmers (farmers who produced things like wheat, dairy products, tobacco and corn) to leave their fields fallow in order to end agricultural surpluses and boost prices.

June's National Industrial Recovery Act guaranteed that workers would have the right to unionize and bargain collectively for higher wages and better working conditions; it also suspended some antitrust laws and established a federally funded Public Works Administration.

In addition to the Agricultural Adjustment Act, the Tennessee Valley Authority Act, and the National Industrial Recovery Act, Roosevelt had won passage of 12 other major laws, including the Glass-Steagall Act (an important banking bill) and the Home Owners' Loan Act, in his first 100 days in office.

Almost every American found something to be pleased about and something to complain about in this motley collection of bills, but it was clear to all that FDR was taking the "direct, vigorous" action that he'd promised in his inaugural address.

Despite the best efforts of President Roosevelt and his cabinet, however, the Great Depression continued—the nation's economy continued to wheeze; unemployment persisted; and people grew angrier and more desperate. So, in the spring of 1935, Roosevelt launched a second, more aggressive series of federal programs, sometimes called the Second New Deal.

In April, he created the Works Progress Administration (WPA) to provide jobs for unemployed people. WPA projects weren't allowed to compete with private industry, so they focused on building things like post offices, bridges, schools, highways and parks. The WPA also gave work to artists, writers, theater directors and musicians.

In July 1935, the National Labor Relations Act, also known as the Wagner Act, created the National Labor Relations Board to supervise union elections and prevent businesses from treating their workers unfairly. In August, FDR signed the Social Security Act of 1935, which guaranteed pensions to millions of Americans, set up a system of unemployment insurance and stipulated that the federal government would help care for dependent children and the disabled.

In 1936, while campaigning for a second term, FDR told a roaring crowd at Madison Square Garden that "The forces of 'organized money' are unanimous in their hate for me—and I welcome their hatred."

He went on: "I should like to have it said of my first Administration that in it the forces of selfishness and of lust for power met their match, [and] I should like to have it said of my second Administration that in it these forces have met their master."

This FDR had come a long way from his earlier repudiation of class-based politics and was promising a much more aggressive fight against the people who were profiting from the Depression-era troubles of ordinary Americans. He won the election by a landslide.'[41]

While all this seems very positive, the change was slow in coming to the countryside where environmental damage was an additional hazard people

[41] Unknown, 'New Deal', accessed 11/19. https://www.history.com/topics/great-depression/new-deal

had to contend with. It was those left out of the New Deal, who had to migrate for jobs and suffer hardship while others in the cities found their lives improved, that Steinbeck visited and found inspiration from.

John Steinbeck

Enter into our scene John Ernst Steinbeck Jr, born in 1902 and rising to adulthood in the middle of this turbulent period of American history. He was a complex man who held contradictory and sometimes confusingly dissonant views, but made a huge mark on the history of American literature. Here's how he described himself:

'Among the generality of men I am tall—six feet even—although among the males of my family I am considered a dwarf. They range from six feet two inches to six feet five, and I know that both my sons, when they stretch their full height, will overtop me. I am very wide of shoulder and, in the condition I now find myself[42], narrow of hip. My legs are long in proportion to my trunk and are said to be shapely. My hair is a grizzled grey, my eyes blue and my cheeks ruddy, a complexion inherited from my Irish mother. My face has not ignored the passage of time, but recorded it with scars, lines, furrows, and erosions.' [43]

---

[42] He's referring to his age, as he wrote this passage aged 58 and considered himself an old man.

[43] Steinbeck, John (1997 ed), *Travels with Charley*, UK: Penguin, 32.

Born to a middle class family in Salinas, California (and it's not a coincidence that his writing is set mostly in this region), Steinbeck recalled this time well, despite his protestations.

'Early memories of Salinas are so confused in my mind that I don't know, actually, what I remember and what I was told I remember. I am fairly clear on the earthquake in 1906. My father took me down Main Street and I remember brick buildings, spilled outward. Our own wooden house was not injured, but the chimney had completely turned around without falling...

[In terms of the population], There were two thousand five hundred people in Salinas then, but boosters confidently predicted it would someday be a metropolis of five thousand. Tradition was strong in Salinas and my town never forgot nor forgave an injury . . .

Salinas was never a pretty town. It took a darkness from the swamps. The high grey fog hung over it and the ceaseless wind blew up the valleys, cold and with a kind of desolate monotony. The mountains on both sides of the valley were beautiful, but Salinas was not and we knew it. Perhaps that is why a kind of violent assertiveness, and energy like the compensation for sin grew up in the town.'[44]

In some ways Steinbeck had a difficult childhood, even though it was economically safe. His mother had strong aspirations for her son, but was also very critical of him. One of their neighbours later recalled:

'Mrs Steinbeck was always despairing about her son, trying to get him to achieve more than he did. She saw his brilliance and recognised his abilities, but found his misbehaviour, and tendencies to be a loner, exasperating. It

[44] Steinbeck, John (2003), *America and Americans,* USA: Viking Penguin, 4.

seemed to her that he should be doing better work in school and should be more obedient at home. She pushed him to join clubs and church organisations, but he wasn't very willing. And sometimes he would defy her and ▮▮▮ back. She often said he would either get to the White House as president or go to jail.' [45]

His father was not the role model John wanted either. Despite being an upright and thrifty citizen of Salinas, he was not a good manager and his flour milling business collapsed. John Ernst[46] then sunk into a deep depression but tried his hand at running an animal feed store, only for cars and machinery to rapidly replace horses in their role on the farm, so this business failed too. The Steinbecks became supported by their community throughout hard times. Another Salinas resident recalled:

'People pulled together in those days like they don't do now. I don't think it's easy to remember now, but everyone was a pioneer then; we realised if one man fell, everyone would fall. You helped your neighbour . . .there was no sense of one man out for himself.' [47]

Despite John's feelings towards his parents, the Steinbecks were a close family and he and his sisters were in constant correspondence throughout his life.

As John progressed through high school he developed a love of writing and it was clear that he was talented. Personally he became very insecure about his looks and took family nicknames like 'muskrat' to heart, and this dislike of

---

[45] Quoted in Parini, Jay (1994), *John Steinbeck, A Biography*, UK: Heinemann, 24.

[46] Steinbeck's father will be referred to by this name to differentiate him from his son.

[47] Quoted in Parini, *Steinbeck*, 21.

how he looked would carry on until old age.[48] Aged ten, his aunt gifted him a book about King Arthur which greatly inspired him and gave him a love of legends which he held throughout his life. It was not an easy read by any means. This extract from the book he was gifted will give you an idea of the kind of texts he was able to tackle at a primary school age:

'The meanwhile as this was a-doing, in came Merlin to King Mark, and seeing all his doing, said, Here shall be in this same place the greatest battle betwixt two knights that was or ever shall be, and the truest lovers, and yet none of them shall slay other. And there Merlin wrote their names upon the tomb with letters of gold that should fight in that place, whose names were Launcelot de Lake, and Tristram. Thou art a marvellous man, said King Mark unto Merlin, that speakest of such marvels, thou art a boistous man and an unlikely to tell of such deeds. What is thy name? said King Mark. At this time, said Merlin, I will not tell, but at that time when Sir Tristram is taken with his sovereign lady, then ye shall hear and know my name, and at that time ye shall hear tidings that shall not please you. Then said Merlin to Balin, Thou hast done thyself great hurt, because that thou savest not this lady that slew herself, that might have saved her an thou wouldest. By the faith of my body, said Balin, I might not save her, for she slew herself suddenly. Me repenteth, said Merlin; because of the death of that lady thou shalt strike a stroke most dolorous that ever man struck, except the stroke of our Lord, for thou shalt hurt the truest knight and the man of most worship that now liveth, and through that stroke three kingdoms shall be in great poverty, misery and wretchedness twelve years, and the knight shall not be whole of that wound for many years. Then Merlin took his leave of Balin. And Balin said, If I wist it were sooth that ye say I should do such a perilous deed as that, I would slay myself to make thee a liar. Therewith Merlin vanished away suddenly. And then Balan and his brother took their leave of King Mark. First, said the king, tell me your name.

---

[48] Towards the end of his life, John embraced his appearance and wore eccentric clothes to accentuate it.

Sir, said Balan, ye may see he beareth two swords, thereby ye may call him
the Knight with the Two Swords. And so departed King Mark unto Camelot to
King Arthur, and Balin took the way toward King Rience; and as they rode
together they met with Merlin disguised, but they knew him not. Whither ride
you? said Merlin. We have little to do, said the two knights, to tell thee. But
what is thy name? said Balin. At this time, said Merlin, I will not tell it thee. It is
evil seen, said the knights, that thou art a true man that thou wilt not tell thy
name. As for that, said Merlin, be it as it be may, I can tell you wherefore ye
ride this way, for to meet King Rience; but it will not avail you without ye have
my counsel. Ah! said Balin, ye are Merlin; we will be ruled by your counsel.
Come on, said Merlin, ye shall have great worship, and look that ye do
knightly, for ye shall have great need. As for that, said Balin, dread you not,
we will do what we may.' [49]

His reputation as a writer only increased throughout high school. One
classmate in the year below Steinbeck recalled:

'I don't think John stood out particularly in high school . . . not until the very
end, in fact. But everyone knew him and liked him. His sister, Mary was
more popular. John was known as a writer even then. He would get you into
a corner and spin a hell of a yarn. From what people said to me at the time,
he wrote a good bit of the yearbook all by himself. It just didn't surprise any
of us when he became famous for his books. It all made sense.' [50]

When the time came, Steinbeck fulfilled his mother's ambitions for him to
attend university and enrolled at Stanford to study English. He hated it. John
just wanted to write without any criticism and hated grinding out essays, and

---

[49] Thomas Malory, *'Le Morte D'Arthur'*, accessed 10/19. https://www.gutenberg.org/files/
1251/1251-h/1251-h.htm. The lack of punctuation and spacing is as it was written in the print
version.

[50] Quoted in Parini, *Steinbeck*, 31.

he dropped out in 1925 without completing his degree. He travelled around, doing a variety of odd jobs including a caretaker of a country house and working at a fish hatchery, and finally moved to San Francisco in 1928 without a penny in his pocket to try and impress a girl he had met on holiday. His sister remembered this time in Steinbeck's life positively.

'He never minded being down and out. I think he actually liked it. Young writers were supposed to be poor.'[51]

Here is a good point to pause the narrative of Steinbeck's life to examine his politics, because it was in San Francisco that his future wife, Carol, began to invite Steinbeck to left-wing political meanings. The debate about whether Steinbeck was a communist still rages today, with the Independent naming him as one of their top Marx-influenced writers in 2018.

'Steinbeck's crowning achievement is undoubtedly The Grapes of Wrath (1939), for which he won the Pulitzer Prize. Its protagonist, Tom Joad, is an Oklahoma farm hand driven out of the Dust Bowl with his family and thousands of others by economic hardship to seek a new life in the Promised Land of the west coast.

The strength of the novel—famously filmed by John Ford in 1940 starring Henry Fonda as Joad—lies in its profound sympathy for its working-class characters and outrage at the indignities inflicted upon them by the "greedy bastards" responsible for bringing America to its knees during the Wall Street Crash of 1929.

Folk troubadour Woody Guthrie, a fellow "Okie" with the proto-punk slogan "This Machine Kills Fascists" emblazoned upon his guitar, closely identified

---

[51] Quoted in Parini, *Steinbeck*, 103.

with the book and wrote both a song about Joad and an album called Dust Bowl Ballads in 1940.

Bob Dylan, Bruce Springsteen, Billy Bragg and many others have all since followed his example in bringing popular protest against matters of social injustice to the mainstream.' [52]

In fact, in a bizarre turn of events, he was named by George Orwell on a list of potential communists, despite having never met him.

'Why did George Orwell put John Steinbeck's name on the list of "crypto-communists" he kept in his notebook while writing 1984, his Cold War classic about totalitarian England under a Stalinesque Big Brother? As the troubled alliance between the USSR and the Free World collapsed following World War II, confirming Orwell's deepest doubts and deadliest anxieties about Stalinist dictatorship, Steinbeck was living alone in California, dealing with personal depression, divorce, and the death of Ed Ricketts, while Orwell worked frantically to finish 1984 on a remote island in Scotland, filling his notebook with the names of public figures he considered potential collaborators in the Stalinist invasion he feared.

In their personal lives and political views Orwell and Steinbeck weren't so different. . . [and] Both did their part in the world war against fascism using their best weapon—words.

Like George Orwell, John Steinbeck was an urban liberal activist with small-town conservative roots. . . Yet George Orwell—a communist-inspired

---

[52] Joe Sommerlad, *'Karl Marx at 200: Ten Left Wing writers following in the footsteps of a giant'*, accessed 11/19. https://www.independent.co.uk/arts-entertainment/books/features/karl-marx-200-years-anniversary-left-wing-novelists-george-orwell-hg-wells-john-steinbeck-a8333991.html

socialist with political views left of Steinbeck's—accused Steinbeck of being the communist when the Cold War began. What change caused this charge? Part of the answer can be explained by certain elements of Orwell's peculiar personality—extreme partisanship, English parochialism, and literary pique. As a professional book reviewer, Orwell disparaged American writing, including Steinbeck's. His English pride was hurt by America's rising dominance following World War I and Roosevelt's treatment of Churchill in the closing days of World War II. His political partisanship led to paranoid illusions about the motives of opponents, particularly those within his own party. But there were more likely American writers for George Orwell accuse of being fifth-columnists for communism in the United States.' [53]*

What was the issue with being a Communist in the 1930s? It's the equivalent of saying 'what is the issue with being in ISIS?' today. Communism was un-American, dangerous and foreign. With the Cold War beginning to spread its icy tendrils through the world, being a communist meant being a threat, a spy, and a destabilising influence which could lurk round any corner.

Steinbeck vehemently denied this accusation, of course, in his idiosyncratic and slightly egotistical way.

'I read a piece about myself recently written to reassure my readers that I am not a revolutionary. At the same time the Communist Party denounces me in the same terms. I hasten to inform both the extreme right and the pseudo right which calls itself left that they are both wrong. I am a very dangerous revolutionary. . .

[53] William Ray, *'Why did George Orwell name Steinbeck a Communist?'*, accessed 11/19. http://www.steinbecknow.com/2013/09/19/george-orwell-steinbeck-communist/

Me and my work they do not like and have eliminated where they have the power. My books are forbidden entrance to Soviet centres not because they are not truly revolutionary but because they are. Indeed, any criticism is construed as a revolt by the two great wings of reaction' [54]

His thoughts started to take a more philosophical turn. One of his more interesting ideas was the idea of the Phalanx, which he explained in a letter to a friend:

'We know that with certain arrangements of atoms we might have what we call a bar of iron. Certain other arrangements of atoms plus a mysterious principle make a living cell. Now the living cell is very sensitive to outside stimuli or tropisms. [55] *A further arrangement of cells and a very complex one may make a unit which we call a man. That has been our final union. But there have been mysterious things which could not be explained if man is the final unit. He also arranges himself into larger units, which I have called the phalanx. The phalanx has its own memory—memory of the great tides when the moon was close, memory of starvations when the good of the world was exhausted. Memories of methods when numbers of the units had to be destroyed for the good of the whole, memory of the history of itself.'* [56]

According to Steinbeck, this would mean that as a civilisation we all share a sort of collective memory since this Phalanx represents our society. Later critics have examined this idea further:

'His theory is that there is a difference between the individual on his own and as part of a group. Since the group is a unit often with a drive, an intent, an

---

[54] Steinbeck, *America and Americans*, 89.

[55] Turning around in reaction to a stimuli. An example is a Venus flytrap closing on a fly.

[56] Quoted in Parini, *Steinbeck*, 174.

end, a method, a reaction which in no way resembles the same things possessed by the men who make [it] up. Steinbeck defined such groups as greater beasts controlling [their] unit—men with an iron discipline. The essay was influenced by the period when it was written. The world was going through great changes, with the rise in Italy, Germany, and Japan of totalitarian governments which subordinated the individual to the State; industrial unionism and the growth of large cities furthermore encouraged mass movements. [57]

So, maybe, we are all Lennie and George and Curley and Crooks.

The 1920s and 1930s were not a great time for Steinbeck's writing as he lost his mother to illness and his first marriage broke up due to infidelity.[58] In these wilderness years he took to the countryside and found inspiration, as he later mentioned in a letter to a friend.

'I think I would like to write the story of this whole valley, of all the little towns and all the farms and the ranches in the wider hills. I can see how I would like to do it so that it would be the valley of the world.' [59]

In the breakup of his marriage, and after some journalistic gigs writing about the effects of the Great Depression[60] Steinbeck produced Of Mice and Men, the short novella that catapulted him to the mainstream and made him a marketable author. He hated publicity but did use his fame to good effect, such as asking for meetings with the President to suggest how propaganda

---

[57] Marcia Salazar, *'John Steinbeck's Phalanx Theory'*, accessed 11/19. https://periodicos.ufsc.br/index.php/desterro/article/viewFile/8798/9820..

[58] He actually reached an agreement with his wife's boyfriend in which they both shook hands and agreed that the boyfriend could pursue a relationship with her.

[59] Parini, *John Steinbeck*, 172.

[60] More on these later…

could be put to good use in the Second World War. He started the family he had long hoped for while he was poor after meeting Gwen (his second wife) and raising two sons with her. He worked in Hollywood, turning his novels into scripts, and visited the people of Russia and Ukraine in an attempt to share their stories in the same way he had with the American poor. His second marriage turned into a bitter divorce and he found love, finally, with his third wife, Elaine. Through mighty works like East of Eden and The Grapes of Wrath, and pushing through periods of depression and alcoholism, he managed to achieve the greatest honour for a writer. His Nobel Prize acceptance speech is a lovely final note in this summary of his career.

'Such is the prestige of the Nobel award and of this place where I stand that I am impelled, not to squeak like a grateful and apologetic mouse, but to roar like a lion out of pride in my profession and in the great and good men who have practiced it through the ages.

Literature was not promulgated by a pale and emasculated critical priesthood singing their litanies in empty churches—nor is it a game for the cloistered elect, the tinhorn mendicants of low calorie despair.

Literature is as old as speech. It grew out of human need for it, and it has not changed except to become more needed.

The skalds[61], the bards[62], the writers are not separate and exclusive. From the beginning, their functions, their duties, their responsibilities have been decreed by our species.

---

[61] Ancient Viking storytellers.

[62] Medieval storytellers.

Humanity has been passing through a gray and desolate time of confusion. My great predecessor, William Faulkner, speaking here, referred to it as a tragedy of universal fear so long sustained that there were no longer problems of the spirit, so that only the human heart in conflict with itself seemed worth writing about.

Faulkner, more than most men, was aware of human strength as well as of human weakness. He knew that the understanding and the resolution of fear are a large part of the writer's reason for being.

This is not new. The ancient commission of the writer has not changed. He is charged with exposing our many grievous faults and failures, with dredging up to the light our dark and dangerous dreams for the purpose of improvement.

Furthermore, the writer is delegated to declare and to celebrate man's proven capacity for greatness of heart and spirit—for gallantry in defeat—for courage, compassion and love.

In the endless war against weakness and despair, these are the bright rally-flags of hope and of emulation.

I hold that a writer who does not passionately believe in the perfectibility of man, has no dedication nor any membership in literature.

The present universal fear has been the result of a forward surge in our knowledge and manipulation of certain dangerous factors in the physical world.

It is true that other phases of understanding have not yet caught up with this great step, but there is no reason to presume that they cannot or will not draw abreast. Indeed it is a part of the writer's responsibility to make sure that they do.

With humanity's long proud history of standing firm against natural enemies, sometimes in the face of almost certain defeat and extinction, we would be cowardly and stupid to leave the field on the eve of our greatest potential victory.

Understandably, I have been reading the life of Alfred Nobel—a solitary man, the books say, a thoughtful man. He perfected the release of explosive forces, capable of creative good or of destructive evil, but lacking choice, ungoverned by conscience or judgment.

Nobel saw some of the cruel and bloody misuses of his inventions. He may even have foreseen the end result of his probing—access to ultimate violence —to final destruction. Some say that he became cynical, but I do not believe this. I think he strove to invent a control, a safety valve. I think he found it finally only in the human mind and the human spirit. To me, his thinking is clearly indicated in the categories of these awards.

They are offered for increased and continuing knowledge of man and of his world—for understanding and communication, which are the functions of literature. And they are offered for demonstrations of the capacity for peace – the culmination of all the others.

Less than fifty years after his death, the door of nature was unlocked and we were offered the dreadful burden of choice.

We have usurped many of the powers we once ascribed to God.
Fearful and unprepared, we have assumed lordship over the life or death of
the whole world—of all living things.

The danger and the glory and the choice rest finally in man. The test of his
perfectibility is at hand.

Having taken Godlike power, we must seek in ourselves for the responsibility
and the wisdom we once prayed some deity might have.

Man himself has become our greatest hazard and our only hope.

So that today, St. John the apostle may well be paraphrased …
In the end is the Word, and the Word is Man—and the Word is with Men.' [63]

---

[63] John Steinbeck, *'Nobel Prize Acceptance Speech'*, accessed 11/19. https://
www.nobelprize.org/prizes/literature/1962/steinbeck/25229-john-steinbeck-banquet-
speech-1962/

Something that happened

Steinbeck is said to be the king of American Protest Writing, so when we discuss Of Mice and Men it's important to place him within that tradition. We will need a definition of Protest Writing to begin with.

'The definition of "protest literature" is fluid having different connotations for different people. According to the deconstructionists all literary writing is ultimately a form of protest. For the social and historical critics literary protests must contain a specific political aim, such as changing a law while for a marxist literary protest should disturb the social order in terms of the relationship between social classes. A feminist critic might argue that protest does or does not promote a gender bias and a psychologist might see literary protest as a manifestation of the subconscious. Social protest may take an altogether new form for a traditional literary critic who might argue that the moral relationship between aesthetics and the political message is the content of protest literature. Protest Literature has existed in different forms throughout literary history. Some of the greatest writers in history have employed their talents toward awakening the public to injustices locally and world wide. It has in its gamut some of the most stirring, thought provoking and inciting writings on the struggle of humanity against social injustice. ▮▮▮▮▮▮▮ *focuses on revealing society's ills and literature [and] advocates or opposes certain types of social or political reform.'* [64]

There absolutely was a real setting which inspired the action of Of Mice and Men. On his summer holidays from university Steinbeck worked at a ranch owned by a sugar company his father had begun to work for. They mostly cultivated sugar beet, but some diversified into beef cattle, hay and alfalfa.

---

[64] Unknown, *'Protest Literature: Some Considerations'*, accessed 12/19. https://shodhganga.inflibnet.ac.in/bitstream/10603/135784/6/06_chapter%201.pdf

'Each ranch had a permanent staff, but during certain times of the year itinerant ranch hands were hired. These were the 'bindlestiffs' who eventually became the subject of Steinbeck's Of Mice and Men: broken men who wandered the countryside looking for a bit of work on this or that farm. They would do anything—buck barley[65], feed the pigs, dig wells, harvest fruit or vegetables, mend fences.'[66]

While this was very much alive in Steinbeck's memory, perhaps it was his journalistic trips to California in 1936 to document the lives of migrant workers which sparked the creative process of Of Mice and Men.

'In August, 1936, after Lange's Migrant Mother images[67] had been published to a gratifyingly large public response, the [San Francisco] News sent ███████████████████████████████████ *to produce a series of articles on the migrant labour camps. The series appeared in successive issues from October 5 to October 11 under the running title of 'The Harvest Gypsies'[68]*

Glancing over an extract from a single article is enough to cement the inspiration behind Of Mice and Men to this reporting.

'At this season of the year, when California's great crops are coming into harvest, the heavy grapes, the prunes, the apples and lettuce and the rapidly maturing cotton, our highways swarm with the migrant workers, that shifting group of nomadic, poverty-stricken harvesters driven by hunger and the threat of hunger from crop to crop, from harvest to harvest, up and down the

---

[65] Throwing large sacks of barley onto the back of a truck.

[66] Parini, *Steinbeck*, 42.

[67] The famous photo of the mother holding two children.

[68] Watkins, T H (1993), *The Great Depression: America in the 1930s,* USA: Blackside, 299.

state and into Oregon to some extent, and into Washington a little. But it is California which has and needs the majority of these new gypsies. It is a short study of these wanderers that these articles will undertake. There are at least 150,000 homeless migrants wandering up and down the state, and that is an army large enough to make it important to every person in the state. To the casual traveler on the great highways the movements of the migrants are mysterious if they are seen at all, for suddenly the roads will be filled with open rattletrap cars loaded with children and with dirty bedding, with fire-blackened cooking utensils. The boxcars and gondolas on the railroad lines will be filled with men. And then, just as suddenly, they will have disappeared from the main routes. On side roads and near rivers where there is little travel the squalid, filthy squatters' camp will have been set up, and the orchards will be filled with pickers and cutters and driers.

The unique nature of California agriculture requires that these migrants exist, and requires that they move about. Peaches and grapes, hops and cotton cannot be harvested by a resident population of laborers. For example, a large peach orchard which requires the work of 20 men the year round will need as many as 2000 for the brief time of picking and packing. And if the migration of the 2000 should not occur, if it should be delayed even a week, the crop will rot and be lost.

Thus, in California we find a curious attitude toward a group that makes our agriculture successful. The migrants are needed, and they are hated. Arriving in a district they find the dislike always meted out by the resident to the foreigner, the outlander. This hatred of the stranger occurs in the whole range of human history, from the most primitive village form to our own highly organized industrial farming. The migrants are hated for the following reasons, that they are ignorant and dirty people, that they are carriers of disease, that they increase the necessity for police and the tax bill for schooling in a community, and that if they are allowed to organize they can,

47

simply by refusing to work, wipe out the season's crops. They are never received into a community nor into the life of a community. Wanderers in fact, they are never allowed to feel at home in the communities that demand their services.

Let us see what kind of people they are, where they come from, and the routes of their wanderings. In the past they have been of several races, encouraged to come and often imported as cheap labor; Chinese in the early period, then Filipinos, Japanese and Mexicans. These were foreigners, and as such they were ostracized and segregated and herded about.

If they attempted to organize they were deported or arrested, and having no advocates6 they were never able to get a hearing for their problems. But in recent years the foreign migrants have begun to organize, and at this danger signal they have been deported in great numbers, for there was a new reservoir from which a great quantity of cheap labor could be obtained. The drought in the middle west has driven the agricultural populations of Oklahoma, Nebraska and parts of Kansas and Texas westward. Their lands are destroyed and they can never go back to them.

Thousands of them are crossing the borders in ancient rattling automobiles, destitute and hungry and homeless, ready to accept any pay so that they may eat and feed their children. And this is a new thing in migrant labor, for the foreign workers were usually imported without their children and everything that remains of their old life with them.

They arrive in California usually having used up every resource to get here, even to the selling of the poor blankets and utensils and tools on the way to buy gasoline. They arrive bewildered and beaten and usually in a state of semi-starvation, with only one necessity to face immediately, and that is to find work at any wage in order that the family may eat.

And there is only one field in California that can receive them. Ineligible for relief, they must become migratory field workers.

Because the old kind of laborers, Mexicans and Filipinos, are being deported and repatriated very rapidly, while on the other hand the river of dust bowl refugees increases all the time, it is this new kind of migrant that we shall largely consider.

The earlier foreign migrants have invariably been drawn from a peon class. This is not the case with the new migrants.

They are small farmers who have lost their farms, or farm hands who have lived with the family in the old American way. They are men who have worked hard on their own farms and have felt the pride of possessing and living in close touch with the land.

They are resourceful and intelligent Americans who have gone through the hell of the drought, have seen their lands wither and die and the top soil blow away; and this, to a man who has owned his land, is a curious and terrible pain.

And then they have made the crossing and have seen often the death of their children on the way. Their cars have been broken down and been repaired with the ingenuity of the land man.

Often they patched the worn-out tires every few miles. They have weathered the thing, and they can weather much more for their blood is strong. They are descendants of men who crossed into the middle west, who won their lands by fighting, who cultivated the prairies and stayed with them until they went back to desert.

And because of their tradition and their training, they are not migrants by nature. They are gypsies by force of circumstances.

In their heads, as they move wearily from harvest to harvest, there is one urge and one overwhelming need, to acquire a little land again, and to settle on it and stop their wandering. One has only to go into the squatters' camps where the families live on the ground and have no homes, no beds and no equipment; and one has only to look at the strong purposeful faces, often filled with pain and more often, when they see the corporation-held idle lands, filled with anger, to know that this new race is here to stay and that heed must be taken of it.

It should be understood that with this new race the old methods of repression, of starvation wages, of jailing, beating and intimidation are not going to work; these are American people. Consequently we must meet them with understanding and attempt to work out the problem to their benefit as well as ours.

It is difficult to believe what one large speculative farmer has said, that the success of California agriculture requires that we create and maintain a peon class. For if this is true, then California must depart from the semblance of democratic government that remains here.

The names of the new migrants indicate that they are of English, German and Scandinavian descent. There are Munns, Holbrooks, Hansens, Schmidts. And they are strangely anachronistic in one way: Having been brought up in the prairies where industrialization never penetrated, they have jumped with no transition from the old agrarian, self-containing farm where nearly everything used was raised or manufactured, to a system of agriculture so industrialized that the man who plants a crop does not often see, let alone harvest, the fruit of his planting, where the migrant has no contact with the growth cycle.

And there is another difference between their old life and the new. They have come from the little farm districts where democracy was not only possible but inevitable, where popular government, whether practiced in the Grange, in church organization or in local government, was the responsibility of every man. And they have come into the country where, because of the movement necessary to make a living, they are not allowed any vote whatever, but are rather considered a properly unprivileged class.

Let us see the fields that require the impact of their labor and the districts to which they must travel. As one little boy in a squatters camp said, "When they need us they call us migrants, and when we've picked their crop, we're bums and we got to get out."

There are the vegetable crops of the Imperial Valley, the lettuce, cauliflower, tomatoes, cabbage to be picked and packed, to be hoed and irrigated. There are several crops a year to be harvested, but there is not time distribution sufficient to give the migrants permanent work.

The orange orchards deliver two crops a year, but the picking season is short. Farther north, in Kern County and up the San Joaquin Valley, the migrants are needed for grapes, cotton, pears, melons, beans and peaches.
In the outer valley, near Salinas, Watsonville, and Santa Clara there are lettuce, cauliflowers, artichokes, apples, prunes, apricots. North of San Francisco the produce is of grapes, deciduous fruits and hops. The Sacramento Valley needs masses of migrants for its asparagus, its walnuts, peaches, prunes, etc. These great valleys with their intensive farming make their seasonal demands on migrant labor.

A short time, then, before the actual picking begins, there is the scurrying on the highways, the families in open cars hurrying to the ready crops and hurrying to be first at work. For it has been the habit of the growers associations of the state to provide by importation, twice as much labor as was necessary, so that wages might remain low.

Hence the hurry, for if the migrant is a little late the places may all be filled and he will have taken his trip for nothing. And there are many things that may happen even if he is in time. The crop may be late, or there may occur one of those situations like that at Nipomo last year when twelve hundred workers arrived to pick the pea crop only to find it spoiled by rain. All resources having been used to get to the field, the migrants could not move on; they stayed and starved until government aid tardily was found for them.

And so they move, frantically, with starvation close behind them. And in this series of articles we shall try to see how they live and what kind of people they are, what their living standard is, what is done for them and to them, and what their problems and needs are. For while California has been successful in its use of migrant labor, it is gradually building a human structure which will certainly change the State, and may, if handled with the inhumanity and stupidity that have characterized the past, destroy the present system of agricultural economics.' [69]

The question remains as to how much he was part of the poor he saw, and whether he could truly empathise with them. Steinbeck had been poor, true, but he always had the safety net of his family's money. He visited the migrant

---

[69] John Steinbeck, *'The Harvest Gypsies'* (excerpt), accessed 11/19. https://www.commonlit.org/en/texts/excerpt-from-the-harvest-gypsies

workers but in the capacity of a relatively wealthy journalist who had been living off his wife's wages while he tried to write.

Some critics have expressed this rather harshly:

'Most people imagine that Steinbeck came from an impoverished background and was almost one of those workers in The Grapes Of Wrath, but his family home in Salinas was a beautiful Victorian house with maids and servants. His was a self-conscious identification with working people, but he always travelled first-class and stayed in suites at the Dorchester in London and the Georges Cinq in Paris.' [70]

Perhaps his view of the poor is a kind of idealised hero worship, as later critics have pointed out:

'The poor are Steinbeck's heroes not because they have arrived at any superior knowledge or conduct but because they are open, irreverently, to the possibility that there is no moral knowledge at all. They are engaged in, but have not finally resolved, the enduring conflicts between the virtues of society and those of solitude, between an active and contemplative life, between the lure of flesh and the lure of the spirit, between responsibility and freedom.' [71]

Even so, it's widely acknowledged that these experiences in the migrant camps led to Steinbeck writing a draft of a novella called Something That Happened.

---

[70] David Lister, *'Steinbeck: not so saintly: He was a spoilt rich kid who mistreated his wife. David Lister looks at a new biography of the author'*, accessed 11/19. https://www.independent.co.uk/news/uk/home-news/steinbeck-not-so-saintly-he-was-a-spoilt-rich-kid-who-mistreated-his-wife-david-lister-looks-at-a-1431995.html

[71] Quoted in Parini, *Steinbeck*, 199.

'This deliberately nondescript title was intended to remove any sense of individual blame for the events that occur in the novella.' [72]

It also shows the futility of George's struggle, since Lennie's death was simply something that happened.

The poem that inspired a change in title was 'To A Mouse' by Robert Burns, alleged read to Steinbeck by his wife and best friend. It was written after the poet noticed that he had destroyed a mouse's nest while mowing grass and caused him to reflect on how he ruined the mouse's plans for safety. Burns was proud of his Scottish nationality and wrote as he would say the poem in his accent.

'Wee, sleekit, cowran, tim'rous beastie,
O, what a panic's in thy breastie!
Thou need na start awa sae hasty,
Wi' bickering brattle!
I wad be laith to rin an' chase thee,
Wi' murd'ring pattle!

I'm truly sorry Man's dominion
Has broken Nature's social union,
An' justifies that ill opinion,
Which makes thee startle,
At me, thy poor, earth-born companion,
An' fellow-mortal!

I doubt na, whyles, but thou may thieve;
What then? poor beastie, thou maun live!

---

[72] Unknown, *'Five Fascinating Facts about Of Mice and Men'*, accessed 11/19. https://interestingliterature.com/2015/10/07/five-fascinating-facts-about-of-mice-and-men/

A daimen-icker in a thrave 'S a sma' request:
I'll get a blessin wi' the lave,
An' never miss't!
Thy wee-bit housie, too, in ruin!
It's silly wa's the win's are strewin!
An' naething, now, to big a new ane,
O' foggage green!
An' bleak December's winds ensuin,
Baith snell an' keen!

Thou saw the fields laid bare an' wast,
An' weary Winter comin fast,
An' cozie here, beneath the blast,
Thou thought to dwell,
Till crash! the cruel coulter past
Out thro' thy cell.

That wee-bit heap o' leaves an' stibble,
Has cost thee monie a weary nibble!
Now thou's turn'd out, for a' thy trouble,
But house or hald.
To thole the Winter's sleety dribble,
An' cranreuch cauld!

But Mousie, thou are no thy-lane,
In proving foresight may be vain:
*The best laid schemes **o' Mice an' Men**[73],*
Gang aft agley,

---

[73] My emphasis.

An' lea'e us nought but grief an' pain,
For promis'd joy!

Still, thou art blest, compar'd wi' me!
The present only toucheth thee:
But Och! I backward cast my e'e,
On prospects drear!
An' forward, tho' I canna see,
I guess an' fear!' [74]

Other than that one line, the links between this poem and the narrative in the novella are deeper than it first appears.

'In the poem, Burns concludes, 'The best laid schemes o' mice an 'men / Gang aft agley—i.e., 'go often awry'. The lines are often misremembered and misquoted (or, if you will, adapted) as 'the best laid plans'. But the allusion to the Burns poem neatly sums up Lennie Small's personality in the novel: he is kind to animals but doesn't realise his own strength, and often unintentionally ends up killing them (like Burns's mouse).' [75]

Steinbeck designed the novella to be adapted into a play, and towards the end of his life reflected rather harshly on this strategy.

'The book Of Mice and Men was an experiment and, in what it set out to do, it was a failure. . .' [76]

---

[74] Robert Burns, *'To A Mouse'*, accessed 10/19. http://www.robertburns.org.uk/Assets/Poems_Songs/toamouse.htm

[75] Unknown, *'Five Fascinating Facts'*.

[76] Steinbeck, *America*, 155.

Ironically, the plays based on Of Mice and Men have been very popular. What motivated him to try this strategy? In an introduction to a similar and later experiment he said:

'I find it difficult to read plays, and in this I do not find myself alone. The printed play is read almost exclusively by people closely associated with the theatre, by students of the theatre, and by the comparatively small group of readers who are passionately fond of the theatre. The first reason for this form, then, is to provide a play that will be more widely read because it is presented as ordinary fiction, which is a more familiar medium.' [77]

A lover of drama, he wanted to make it accessible to the masses who may not otherwise go and see a production. To make this easier, he deliberately wrote the book in scenes with a single setting for each.

'There must be no entrance into thoughts of a character unless those thoughts are clearly exposed in the dialogue. People cannot wander around geographically unless the writer has provided some physical technique for making such wanderings convincing on stage. The action must be close-built, and something must have happened to the characters when the curtain has been lowered on the final line.' [78]

This completely explains why each chapter has a new setting and a distinct open and close. It also explains why each chapter is set up with a very detailed description of the scenery, such as the description of the bunkhouse at the start of Chapter Two.

---

[77] Quoted in Neil Rathnell, *'When is a Play not a Play?'*, accessed 10/19. https://neilrathmell.com/2016/02/03/when-is-a-play-not-a-play/

[78] Rathnell, *'When is a Play not a Play?'*.

'The bunkhouse was a long, rectangular building. Inside, the walls were whitewashed and the floor unpainted. In three walls there were small, square windows, and in the fourth, a solid door with a wooden latch. Against the walls were eight bunks, five of them made up with blankets and the other three showing their burlap ticking. Over each bunk there was nailed an apple box with the opening forward so that it made two shelves for the personal belongings of the occupant of the bunk. And these shelves were loaded with little articles, soap and talcum powder, razors and those Western magazines ranch men love to read and scoff at and secretly believe. And there were medicines on the shelves, and little vials, combs; and from nails on the box sides, a few neckties. Near one wall there was a black cast-iron stove, its stovepipe going straight up through the ceiling. In the middle of the room stood a big square table littered with playing cards, and around it were grouped boxes for the players to sit on.' [79]

Steinbeck's agents, upon reading Of Mice and Men, did not approve of it, and argued that it was too enclosed a setting for the amount of deaths which occur. Steinbeck entirely disagreed, and in a letter defended it:

'I'm sorry that you do not find the new book as large in subject as it should be. I probably did not make my subject and symbols clear. The microcosm is rather difficult to handle and apparently I did not get it over—the earth longings of a Lennie who was not to represent insanity at all but the inarticulate and powerful yearning of all men.' [80]

Evidently this appeal worked because it was published and instantly became a success. ███████████████████ due to its inclusion in the Book of The

----

[79] Steinbeck, *Of Mice and Men*, 19.

[80] Brian Hoey, *'Nine Fascinating Facts About John Steinbeck's Of Mice and Men'*, accessed 11/19. https://blog.bookstellyouwhy.com/nine-fascinating-facts-about-john-steinbecks-of-mice-and-men

Month Club, a subscription service that delivered a book to readers every four weeks.

Despite his defiance, Steinbeck, ever a mixture of insecure and egotistical, was nervous even before its publication. He wrote in a letter to his friend:

'It is an experiment and it is two-thirds done. There are problems in it, difficult of resolution. But the biggest problem is a resolution of will. The rewards of work are so sickening to me that I do more with this greatest reluctance. The mind and will must concentrate again and to a purpose . . . The idea of building too carefully for an event seems to me to be doing that old human trick of reducing everything to it's simplest design. Now, the designs of lives are not so simple.' [81]

The reviews from the newspapers were mixed. One reporter for The Nation wrote:

'All but one of the persons in Mr Steinbeck's extremely brief novel and subhuman if the range of the world human is understood to coincide with the range thus far established by fiction.' [82]

Since the aim for the entire 'Full Context' series is to place the texts we study at school into their rightful place, it would be remiss not to mention ████████. Of Mice and Men arrives very shortly before The Grapes of Wrath, arguably Steinbeck's greatest work. The similarities between the works are glaring, to say the least. Take the opening of each novel, for example. This is the beginning of The Grapes of Wrath:

[81] Parini, *Steinbeck*, 214.

[82] Quoted in Parini, *Steinbeck,* 228.

'TO THE red country and part of the gray country of Oklahoma, the last rains came gently, and they did not cut the scarred earth. The plows crossed and recrossed the rivulet marks. The last rains lifted the corn quickly and scattered weed colonies and grass along the sides of the roads so that the gray country and the dark red country began to disappear under a green cover. In the last part of May the sky grew pale and the clouds that had hung in high puffs for so long in the spring were dissipated. The sun flared down on the growing corn day after day until a line of brown spread along the edge of each green bayonet. The clouds appeared, and went away, and in a while they did not try any more. The weeds grew darker green to protect themselves, and they did not spread any more. The surface of the earth crusted, a thin hard crust, and as the sky became pale, so the earth became pale, pink in the red country and white in the gray country. In the water-cut gullies the earth dusted down in dry little streams. Gophers and ant lions started small avalanches. And as the sharp sun struck day after day, the leaves of the young corn became less stiff and erect; they bent in a curve at first, and then, as the central ribs of strength grew weak, each leaf tilted downward. Then it was June, and the sun shone, more fiercely. The brown lines on the corn leaves widened and moved in on the central ribs. The weeds frayed and edged back toward their roots. The air was thin and the sky more pale; and every day the earth paled.' [83]*

Compare the above beautiful opening to the start of Of Mice and Men:

'A few miles south of Soledad, the Salinas River drops in close to the hillside bank and runs deep and green. The water is warm too, for it has slipped twinkling over the yellow sands in the sunlight before reaching the narrow pool. On one side of the river the golden foothill slopes curve up to the strong

---

[83] Steinbeck, John (2017 ed), *The Grapes of Wrath*, UK: Penguin, 3.

and rocky Gabilan Mountains, but on the valley side the water is lined with trees- willows fresh and green with every spring, carrying in their lower leaf junctures the debris of the winter's flooding; and sycamores with mottled, white, recumbent limbs and branches that arch over the pool. On the sandy bank under the trees the leaves lie deep and so crisp that a lizard makes a great skittering if he runs among them. Rabbits come out of the brush to sit on the sand in the evening, and the damp flats are covered with the night tracks of 'coons, and with the spread pads of dogs from the ranches, and with the split-wedge tracks of deer that come to drink in the dark. There is a path through the willows and among the sycamores, a path beaten hard by boys coming down from the ranches to swim in the deep pool, and beaten hard by tramps who come wearily down from the highway in the evening to jungle-up near water. In front of the low horizontal limb of a giant sycamore there is an ash pile made by many fires; the limb is worn smooth by men who have sat on it.'[84]

It's almost like Steinbeck had a checklist which he stuck to, focusing in on the landscape before drawing in to the lives of the people who live there. Despite vast sales when being published, Of Mice and Men remains a source of controversy today.

'Despite the novel's popularity, Of Mice and Men is—officially—the fourth most challenged book in America. According to the American Library Association in 2006, Of Mice and Men is the fourth most controversial book in the United States—'controversial' in that it is one of the most challenged titles in schools and libraries, a book that many people want removed from public libraries. Of Mice and Men has been challenged largely because of the language used in the book—its use of 'vulgar profanity'—but also for a whole host of other perceived taboo issues: 'promoting euthanasia' and being 'anti-

---

[84] Steinbeck, Of Mice and Men, 1.

business' among the more unusual. What constitutes a 'challenge' to a book? According to the Library Association, 'Challenges are defined as formal, written complaints filed with a library or school requesting that materials be removed because of content or appropriateness.' [85]

Since the novella was designed to be turned into a stage play, we need to think about how it has been adapted in this form, since this is exactly what Steinbeck wanted. The first Broadway director to take on the challenge was very keen to offer his opinion to Steinbeck.

'It is only the second act that seems to me to need fresh invention. You have the two natural scenes for it—bunkhouse and the negro's room, but I think the girl should come into both these scenes, and that the fight between Lennie and Curley, which will climax Act 2, must be over the girl. I think the girl should have a scene with Lennie before he kills her. The girl, I think, should be drawn more full: She is the motivating force of the whole thing and should loom larger.' [86]

One quick search online shows many, many productions of Of Mice and Men currently being performed in the UK, perhaps showing the popularity and success of this experiment. Still, Steinbeck's idea of the play novella is just as divisive as it ever was, as a theatre review in 2001 shows.

'The difficulty here is the adaptation itself, which raises questions about the whole issue of page-to-stage adaptations—why do them unless they are more than just a quick substitute for reading the book? This version (for which nobody is credited, so maybe Steinbeck did it himself) is faithful to the novel, offers us both characters and motivations, and bowls along. You certainly

---

[85] Unknown, *'Five Fascinating Facts'*.

[86] Parini, *Steinbeck*, 231.

come away knowing the story, but you don't come away with any richer an experience than if you had stayed at home with the novel. There are simply not enough good reasons why these two and a half hours are in theatrical form.' [87]

[87] Lyn Gardner, *'Of Mice and Men: Birmingham Rep'*, accessed 11/19. https://www.theguardian.com/stage/2001/nov/17/theatre.artsfeatures1

George and Lennie

First, to answer a question commonly asked by innumerable students across the UK: Why do they talk like that?

Steinbeck always aimed to make his characters authentic and based the way he wrote their dialogue on the way the people around him spoke. This was not laziness, but a love of language and changing dialects.

'One of my purposes was to listen, to hear speech, accent, speech rhythms, overtones and emphasis. For speech is so much more than words and sentences.' [88]

One of the fabulous aspects of writing about a modern book is that the writer frequently tells the media their own context, and in an interview following the publication of Of Mice and Men Steinbeck revealed that Lennie had a direct inspiration.

'Lennie was a real person. He's in an insane asylum in California right now. I worked alongside him for many weeks. He didn't kill a girl. He killed a ranch foreman. Got sore because the boss had fired his pal and stuck a pitchfork right through his stomach. I hate to tell you how many times. I saw him do it. We couldn't stop him until it was too late.' [89]

This memory might explain the pitchfork hanging like the sword of Damocles at the start of chapter five, even though Steinbeck's anecdote can't be verified.

---

[88] Steinbeck, *Travels with Charley*, 82.

[89] Quoted in Parini, *Steinbeck*, 43.

'One end of the great barn was piled high with new hay and over the pile hung the four-taloned Jackson fork suspended from its pulley.' [90]

An interesting lens through which to view George and Lennie's relationship is through the parable of Cain and Abel from the Old Testament.

'Adam made love to his wife Eve, and she became pregnant and gave birth to Cain. She said, "With the help of the Lord I have brought forth a man." Later she gave birth to his brother Abel.

Now Abel kept flocks, and Cain worked the soil. In the course of time Cain brought some of the fruits of the soil as an offering to the Lord. And Abel also brought an offering— fat portions from some of the firstborn of his flock. The Lord looked with favor on Abel and his offering, but on Cain and his offering he did not look with favor. So Cain was very angry, and his face was downcast.

Then the Lord said to Cain, "Why are you angry? Why is your face downcast? If you do what is right, will you not be accepted? But if you do not do what is right, sin is crouching at your door; it desires to have you, but you must rule over it."

Now Cain said to his brother Abel, "Let's go out to the field." While they were in the field, Cain attacked his brother Abel and killed him.
Then the Lord said to Cain, "Where is your brother Abel?"
"I don't know," he replied. "Am I my brother's keeper?"
The Lord said, "What have you done? Listen! Your brother's blood cries out to me from the ground. Now you are under a curse and driven from the ground, which opened its mouth to receive your brother's blood from your

---

[90] Steinbeck, *Of Mice and Men*, 64.

hand. When you work the ground, it will no longer yield its crops for you. You will be a restless wanderer on the earth."' [91]

This curse placed upon Cain is played out throughout the action and dialogue of Of Mice and Men. Take the beginning of Slim and George's conversation, for instance.

'Slim moved back slightly so the light was not on his face. "Funny how you an' him string along together." It was Slim's calm invitation to confidence. "What's funny about it?" George demanded defensively. "Oh, I dunno. Hardly none of the guys ever travel together. I hardly never seen two guys travel together.'

This is the mistrust element of the parable playing out in the 'real life' setting of the bunkhouse. William Goldhurst argues that Candy and Crooks joining the plan to buy the farm represents the moment that the curse might be broken:

'This is the high point of optimism as regards the main theme of the story; this is the point when the a possible reversal of the curse of Cain seems most likely, as Steinbeck suggests that the answer to the Lord's question might be 'Yes, I am my brother's keeper.' [92]

Ultimately though, there is no escaping from the curse and therefore the Dream can never really happen.

'Actually the plan is doomed to failure from the beginning; for fraternal living cannot long survive in a world dominated by Aloneness, homelessness and

---

[91] The Bible (New International Version), *'Genesis 4'*, accessed 10/19. https://www.biblegateway.com/passage/?search=Genesis+4&version=NIV

[92] Benson, Jackson J (ed, 1990), *The Short Novels of John Steinbeck*, USA: Duke University Press, 55.

economic futility which Steinbeck presents as the modern counterpart of Cain's curse.' [93]

Another way to see their relationship is as an adult and a child. Lennie's surname, Small, is the first clue that this is a valid interpretation. Mark Spilka notes that Lennie holds:

'That low threshold between rage and pleasure which we all carry within us to adulthood. But by adulthood we have all learned to take precautions which an idiot never learns to take. The force and readiness of our feelings continue: but through diversions and disguises, through civilised controls, we raise the threshold of reactions. This is the only real difference, emotionally, between Lennie and ourselves.' [94]

Lennie cannot rationally make choices, as a child does, but George can and does make choices for the both of them. What makes this analysis more interesting that idle speculation is how often Steinbeck would return to it in his later writing. East of Eden and The Grapes of Wrath both feature Lennie-like moments where a character acts purely on impulse. It's not a stretch, then, to see Lennie as a prototype for these other characters, a cruder version of other characters' struggle between impulse and control.

---

[93] Benson, *The Short Novels*, 55.

[94] Benson, *The Short Novels*, 67.

Violence and the Landscape

Today, the Salinas Valley bills itself as Steinbeck country. Montgomery is the location of the Steinbeck museum, along with ranches where tourists can visit and experience life as a farmhand. It's still a very beautiful and appealing place, but for Steinbeck it was heaven. This perception of California as a mythical paradise is not exclusive to Steinbeck though. Let's refer back to Woody Guthrie, specifically his song 'Do Re Mi'.

'Lots of folks back East, they say, is leavin' home every day
Beatin' the hot old dusty way to the California line
'Cross the desert sands they roll, gettin' out of that old dust bowl
They think they're goin' to a sugar bowl, but here's what they find
Now, the police at the port of entry say
"You're number fourteen thousand for today"

Oh, if you ain't got the do re mi, folks, you ain't got the do re mi
Why, you better go back to beautiful Texas, Oklahoma, Kansas, Georgia, Tennessee
California is a garden of Eden, a paradise to live in or see
But believe it or not, you won't find it so hot
If you ain't got the do re mi.

You want to buy you a home or a farm, that can't deal nobody harm
Or take your vacation by the mountains or sea
Don't swap your old cow for a car, you better stay right where you are
You better take this little tip from me
'Cause I look through the want ads every day
But the headlines on the papers always say

If you ain't got the do re mi, boys, you ain't got the do re mi

Why, you better go back to beautiful Texas, Oklahoma, Kansas, Georgia, Tennessee

California is a garden of Eden, a paradise to live in or see

But believe it or not, you won't find it so hot

If you ain't got the do re mi.' [95]

This association of the Garden of Eden is not too far-fetched for an analysis.

'Ever fascinated with the mythic dimensions of fictions, Steinbeck played in all his work with the Christian notion of 'fallen man'. . . Louise Owens, a recent critic, notes that the valley settings of these books determines that the stories will take place in a fallen world and the quest for the illusive and illusory Eden will be central thematic significance.' [96]

Maybe it's just because that's where Steinbeck began his own journey, but the landscape is always going to be the mythical Eden.

A standard classroom question may well begin with 'How is the theme of violence…?', and while most readers will spot violence in the novel pretty easily it's not necessarily a constructed theme in the novel. It's more of a reflection on the amount of violence that existed in the society surrounding Steinbeck.

One of the ways in which the average working man expressed his fear and anger at the effects of the Great Depression was to join a union and go on strike. With few, if any, labour laws to protect them, these peaceful protests quickly turned violent when employers and local governments objected to the

---

[95] Woody Guthrie, *'Do Re Mi'*, accessed 10/19. https://genius.com/Woody-guthrie-do-re-mi-lyrics. There's a fabulous version of this covered by Mumford and Sons with Elvis Costello on Youtube.

[96] Parini, *John Steinbeck*, 167.

workers' actions. Royce Briar reported on the longshoreman's[97] strike in 1934, known later as Bloody Thursday for the San Francisco Chronicle.

'Blood ran red in the streets of San Francisco yesterday.
In the darkest day this city has known since April 18, 1906, one thousand embattled police held at bay five thousand longshoremen and their sympathizers in a sweeping front south of Market street and east of Second street.

The furies of street warfare raged for hour piled on hour.
Two were dead, one was dying, 32 others shot and more than three score sent to hospitals.

Hundreds were injured or badly gassed. Still the strikers surged up and down the sunlit streets among thousands of foolhardy spectators. Still the clouds of tear gas, the very air darkened with hurtling bricks. Still the revolver battles. As the middle of the day wore on in indescribable turmoil the savagery of the conflict was in rising crescendo. The milling mobs fought with greater desperation, knowing the troops were coming; the police held to hard-won territory with grim resolution.

It was a Gettysburg[98] in the miniature, with towering warehouses thrown in for good measure. It was one of those days you think of as coming to Budapest. The purpose of it all was this: The State of California had said it would operate its waterfront railroad. The strikers had defied the State of California to do it. The police had to keep them off. They did.

---

[97] A manual labourer who loaded and unloaded cargo from ships, trains or planes. They are also sometimes referred to as 'dockers' or 'stevedores'.

[98] A famous battle in the American Civil War.

Take a San Francisco map and draw a line along Second street south from Market to the bay. It passes over Rincon Hill. That is the west boundary, Market is the north of the battlefield.

Not a street in that big sector but saw its flying lead yesterday, not a street that wasn't tramped by thousands of flying feet as the tide of battle swung high and low, as police drove them back, as they drove police back in momentary victory.

And with a dumbfounding nonchalance, San Franciscans, just plain citizens bent on business, in automobiles and on foot, moved to and fro in the battle area.
Don't think of this as a riot. It was a hundred riots, big and little, first here, now there. Don't think of it as one battle, but as a dozen battles.

It started with a nice, easy swing just as great battles in war often start. The Industrial Association resumed moving goods from Pier 38 at 8 a.m. A few hundred strikers were out, but were held back at Brannan street, as they had been in Tuesday's riot, by the police.

At Bryant and Main streets were a couple of hundred strikers in an ugly mood. Police Captain Arthur de Guire decided to clear them out, and his men went after them with tear gas. The strikers ran, scrambling up Rincon Hill and hurling back rocks.

Proceed now one block away, to Harrison and Main streets. Four policemen are there, about 500 of the mob are on the hill. Those cops looked like fair game.

"Come on, boys," shouted the leaders.

They tell how the lads of the Confederacy had a war whoop that was a holy terror. These boys, a lot of them kids in their teens, came down that hill with a whoop. It sounded blood-curdling. One policeman stood behind a telephone pole to shelter him from the rocks and started firing his revolver.

Up the hill, up Main, came de Guire's men on the run, afoot and the "mounties".[99] A few shots started whizzing from up the hill, just a scattering few, with a high hum like a bumble bee.

Then de Guire's men, about 20 of them, unlimbered from Main and Harrison and fired at random up the hill. The down-plunging mob halted, hesitated, and started scrambling up the hill again.

Here the first man fell, a curious bystander. The gunfire fell away.

Up came the tear gas boys, six or eight carloads of them. They hopped out with their masks on, and the gas guns laid down a barrage on the hillside. The hillside spouted blue gas like the Valley of the Ten Thousand Smokes. Up the hill came the moppers-up, phalanxes of policemen with drawn revolvers. The strikers backed sullenly away on Harrison street, past Fremont street. Suddenly came half a dozen carloads of men from the Bureau of Inspectors, and right behind them a truck load of shotguns and ammunition. In double quick they cleared Rincon Hill. Ten police cars stuck their noses over the brow of the hill.

Noon came. Napoleon said an army travels on its belly. So do strikers and police, and even newspapermen.

---

[99] Police on horseback.

Now it is one o'clock. Rumors of the coming of the soldiery fly across the town. The strikers are massing down at the foot of Mission and Howard streets, where a Belt Line freight train is moving through.

Police are massed there, too; the tear gas squads, the rifle and shotgun men, the mounties. Not a sign of machine guns so far. But the cops have them. There's plenty of talk about the "typewriters."

There they go again into action, the gas boys! They're going up the stubby little streets from the Embarcadero to Steuart street, half blocks up Mission and Howard. Across by the Ferry Building are thousands of spectators. Boom! go the gas guns, boom, boom, boom!

Around the corners, like sheep pouring through a gate, go the rioters, but they don't go very far. They stop at some distance, say a half block away, wipe their eyes a minute, and in a moment comes a barrage of rocks.

Here's the hottest part of the battle from now on, along Steuart street from Howard to Market. No mistake about that. It centers near the I.L.A. headquarters.

See the mounties ride up toward that front of strikers. It's massed across the street, a solid front of men. Take a pair of opera glasses[100] and look at their faces. They are challenging the on-coming mounties. The men in front are kneeling, like sprinters at the mark.

Clatter, clatter, clatter come the bricks. Tinkle goes a window. This is war, boys, and this Steuart street between Howard and Mission is one of the warmest spots American industrial conflict ever saw.

---

[100] Binoculars.

73

The horses rear. The mounted police dodge bricks.

A police gold braid stands in the middle of the street all alone, and he blows his whistle. Up come the gas men, the shotgun men, the rifle men. The rioters don't give way.

Crack and boom! Sounds just like a gas bomb, but no blue smoke this time. Back scrambles the mob and two men lie on the sidewalk. Their blood trickles in a crimson stream away from their bodies.

Over it spreads an air of unutterable confusion. The only organization seems to lie in little squads of officers hurrying hither and yon in automobiles. Sirens keep up a continual screaming in the streets. You can heard them far away. Now it was 2 o'clock. The street battle had gone on for half an hour. How many were shot, no one knew.

Now, it was win or die for the strikers in the next few hours. The time from 2 o'clock to 3 o'clock dragged for police, but went on the wings of the wind for the strikers. An hour's rest. They had to have that one hour.

At 3 o'clock they started again, the fighting surging once more about Steuart and Mission streets. Here was a corner the police had, and had to hold. It was the key to the waterfront, and it was in the shadow of the I.L.A. headquarters.

The rocks started filling the air again. They crashed through street cars. The cars stopped and citizens huddled inside.

Panic gripped the east end of Market street. The ferry crowds were being involved. You thought again of Budapest. The troops were coming. Soldiers. SOLDIERS IN SAN FRANCISCO! WAR IN SAN FRANCISCO!'

This is not an example of conflict journalism from a land far from the readers. This is just a news report on a protest, and a horrifying example of how violence could erupt at a moment's notice in the charged situation of the Great Depression. This tension was widely acknowledged and feared by the elites and the working population alike, as historian Catherine McNichol Stock acknowledges.

'Times of extreme economic and social dislocation create a landscape ripe for political extremism—expressed in both words and deeds. The Great Depression was one of those times, of course, and can still be instructive today.

The "shoot the banker" cry in the Depression did not lead to mass killings but to vicious acts like tarring and feathering.

Faced with the worst economic downturn in history, many local politicians turned the heat up on their rhetoric—particularly in the countryside. For example, the governor of North Dakota, William Langer, a staunch opponent of farm foreclosures, told followers to "shoot the Banker. Treat him like a chicken thief."

That did not mean that farmers all over the northern Plains shot their local bankers. But violence in the impoverished countryside did occur, including the tarring and feathering of a local judge. Across the region, farm leaders also declared a "farm holiday" and local followers attack the men in their communities who chose not to participate.

The long-term loss of employment, land and homes in the 1930s made many in Washington fearful of violence on the left and the right. It was among the reasons why Roosevelt knew that "fear itself" was among the nation's fiercest opponents.'[101]

We also need to remember the fact that Of Mice and Men is set on a farm, the kind of place where meat is more likely to come from an animal you know than a supermarket shelf. Woody Guthrie, political folk singer and migrant worker in the 1930s, wrote the following account in his autobiography, reflecting on when his rural cousin found he had made friends with three stray kittens.

'Warren kicked the loose cotton seed apart.

"Just like tearin' up a bird's nest!" He said. He put the sharp toe of his shoe under the belly of the first little cat, and threw it up against the rock foundation.

"Meoww! Meoww! You little chicken killers! Egg stealers!"

He picked the second kitten up in the grip of his hand, and squeezed til his muscles bulged up. He swung the kitten around, something like a Ferris wheel, as fast as he could turn his arm, and the blood and the entrails of the kitten splashed across the ground, and the sides of the house. Then he held the little body out towards Lawrence[102] and me. We looked at it, and it was just like an empty hide. He threw it away over the fence.'[103]

---

[101] Catherine McNichol Stock, 'Violence in the 1930s', accessed 11/19. https://www.nytimes.com/roomfordebate/2011/01/10/assassins-and-american-history/violence-in-the-1930s

[102] Guthrie's brother.

[103] Guthrie, Woodie (2004 ed), Bound for Glory, UK: Penguin, 80.

Disgusting as this is to us in the twenty-first century, the reality is that Lennie's violence is relatively normal for a rural setting in the early years of the twentieth century.

Of course, we cannot forget that the 1930s were well into the era of mass media. Murders were reported and the illicit thrill of true crime stories was enjoyed by many in the same way we enjoy crime dramas or true crime podcasts today. Just look at the reaction to the notorious 'ladykiller', Harry Powers.

'A con-man calling himself Harry Powers courted wealthy middle-aged widows through matrimonial agencies, and plotted to kill them. He imprisoned and murdered an Illinois widow, her three children, who were 14, 12 and nine, and a Massachusetts divorcee, all of whom came to Quiet Dell willingly.

The crime was the first nationally sensationalised rural serial murder in America. West Virginia native Davis Grubb changed the facts completely for his first novel, The Night of the Hunter. There were no dead children and the seemingly bland, pudgy real-life murderer, who enjoyed his fame but revealed nothing, had become a sham preacher with a gift for terrifying rhetoric. Charles Laughton's famed film adaptation starred Robert Mitchum as the killer.

Viewing the site of the murders became a pilgrimage for thousands from nearby towns and neighbouring states. At the time of his arrest, Powers was writing to more than 200 women. He advanced his correspondences with care, according to phrases culled from romance magazines and the "writings" of Rudolph Valentino; he arranged to meet the woman in question after their letters had "established an understanding" and they planned to marry. Powers ran his advertisement continually in the listings of matrimonial agencies, from the salacious "Cupid's Arrows" to the staid and respectable-sounding

"American Friendship Society". Through the latter, Powers courted Asta Eicher, of Park Ridge, Illinois, Dorothy Lemke, of Northborough, Massachusetts, and dozens of others. He called himself Cornelius Pierson, made promises, and demanded loyalty.

"WEALTHY Widower worth $150,000 with income from $100 to $3,000 per month; civil engineer, and a very fine looking man, of 38, writes: my business enterprises prevent me from making… the acquaintance of the right kind of ladies… Am an Elk and a Mason. Own a beautiful 10-room brick home completely furnished… My wife would have her own car and plenty of spending money. Would have nothing to do but enjoy herself, but she must be strictly a one-man's woman. I would not tolerate infidelity."

Powers called for Eicher in a fine car and took her to "view his properties in the South". He killed her in one of four basement cells he'd constructed in the garage he'd built in Quiet Dell. A week or so later, he returned to Park Ridge for her three children, Grethe, Hart and Annabel. They'd been left in the care of a nursemaid and believed they were going to the home Powers had established with their mother. On the way, "Pierson" was seen buying them ice cream.

The crime took place in a supposedly more innocent time, a Depression-era America in which newspapers and the printed word were still the lifeblood of the nation. In a nation starving for jobs and food, the unfolding saga of Quiet Dell made horrific, compelling copy. Newspapers seized on the "tragedy" as a warning and lesson to women: "Officers point to the fact that Powers picked aged women… because they were susceptible to his amours." Journalists observed that most of his correspondents "had passed… the 'fat and forty' age that women dread". A sensationalistic account written just after his trial, Love Murders of Harry H. Powers, Bluebeard of Quiet Dell, by lawyer Evan

Alan Bartlett, presents the crime as "the most horrible tragedy that has taken place in American annals".

Investigation revealed that Powers had at least three other aliases. He'd moved to Clarksburg only four years before the murders, to marry a local woman he met through a matrimonial agency. She lived above the neighbourhood grocery store she owned with her spinster sister; Powers promptly moved in and renamed it the "Powers Grocery". The two women, fortyish, provided the perfect cover for a con-man murderer. After Powers was jailed, his wife rented the site to a businessman who fenced the property and tried to charge viewers a quarter. Enraged that she tried to profit from the crime, "townsmen" tore down the fence and formed a lynch mob. Police deterred a mob of 2,000 with tear gas and rushed Powers out of town to the State Penitentiary at Moundsville.

The true story was full of metaphor and coincidence simply unbelievable in fiction. The names of the characters alone suggest a dark Victorian fairy tale: the fashionably dressed sheriff was Sheriff Grimm; the judge was Judge Southern; Powers's lawyer was attorney J Ed Law; the principals and jury, during the trial, stayed at the Gore Hotel (as in Al Gore – the hotel belonged to his distant cousins); the desk clerk at the Gore was Truman Parrish. The Clarksburg courthouse was being rebuilt; the accused returned in December 1931 for his trial in the local Opera House. About 1,200 onlookers attended each day, standing in lines around the block to gain entrance.'[104]

Murder and violence in general was exciting to the general public, as it still is today.

---

[104] Jayne Anne Phillips, 'True Crime: America's Most Notorious Ladykiller', accessed 11/19. https://www.telegraph.co.uk/culture/books/10816712/True-crime-Americas-most-notorious-ladykiller.html

A very obvious example of violence in Of Mice and Men is, of course, Curley and Lennie's clash.

'Lennie looked helplessly at George, and then he got up and tried to retreat. Curley was balanced and poised. He slashed at Lennie with his left, and then smashed down his nose with a right. Lennie gave a cry of terror. Blood welled from his nose. "George," he cried. "Make 'um let me alone, George." He backed until he was against the wall, and Curley followed, slugging him in the face. Lennie's hands remained at his sides; he was too frightened to defend himself.

George was on his feet yelling, "Get him, Lennie. Don't let him do it."

Lennie covered his face with his huge paws and bleated with terror. He cried, "Make 'um stop, George." Then Curley attacked his stomach and cut off his wind.

Slim jumped up. "The dirty little rat," he cried, "I'll get 'um myself."

George put out his hand and grabbed Slim. "Wait a minute," he shouted. He cupped his hands around his mouth and yelled, "Get 'im, Lennie!"

Lennie took his hands away from his face and looked about for George, and Curley slashed at his eyes. The big face was covered with blood. George yelled again, "I said get him."

Curley's fist was swinging when Lennie reached for it. The next minute Curley was flopping like a fish on a line, and his closed fist was lost in Lennie's big hand. George ran down the room. "Leggo of him, Lennie. Let go."

But Lennie watched in terror the flopping little man whom he held. Blood ran down Lennie's face, one of his eyes was cut and closed. George slapped him in the face again and again, and still Lennie held on to the closed fist. Curley was white and shrunken by now, and his struggling had become weak. He stood crying, his fist lost in Lennie's paw.

George shouted over and over. "Leggo his hand, Lennie. Leggo. Slim, come help me while the guy got any hand left."

Suddenly Lennie let go his hold. He crouched cowering against the wall. "You tol' me to, George," he said miserably.

Curley sat down on the floor, looking in wonder at his crushed hand. Slim and Carlson bent over him. Then Slim straightened up and regarded Lennie with horror. "We got to get him in to a doctor," he said. "Looks to me like ever' bone in his han' is bust."

"I didn't wanta," Lennie cried. "I didn't wanta hurt him."

Slim said, "Carlson, you get the candy wagon hitched up. We'll take 'um into Soledad an' get 'um fixed up." Carlson hurried out. Slim turned to the whimpering Lennie.
"It ain't your fault," he said. "This punk sure had it comin' to him. But- Jesus! He ain't hardly got no han' left."

Slim hurried out, and in a moment returned with a tin cup of water. He held it to Curley's lips.

George said, "Slim, will we get canned now? We need the stake. Will Curley's old man can us now?"

Slim smiled wryly. He knelt down beside Curley. "You got your senses in hand enough to listen?" he asked. Curley nodded.

"Well, then listen," Slim went on. "I think you got your han' caught in a machine. If you don't tell nobody what happened, we ain't going to. But you jus' tell an' try to get this guy canned and we'll tell ever'body, an' then will you get the laugh."
"I won't tell," said Curley. He avoided looking at Lennie.' [105]

The two features that define Curley are that he's short and he likes boxing. This second feature makes him a very normal man of the era.

'One could say that the 1920's signaled when boxing emerged from the stone ages. The sport's popularity skyrocketed—creating genuine boxing superstars who transcended their sport. The best boxers were among the most famous people in the world and the biggest matches became mega-events. The growing sophistication of motion film cameras helped bring footage to millions, as radios helped spread the good word. This signified the beginning of the golden ages of boxing.

The United States was coming off a momentous victory in World War I. Boxing was able to attract the entertainment dollar with legendary fighters and great fights.

Not all was peaches during this period. First of all, it is impossible to imagine how many future champions were snuffed out by a war with unfathomable numbers of casualties.

---

[105] Steinbeck, *Of Mice and Men*, 70.

While the WWI gave a boost to returning fighters who were championed as war heroes, many a potentially great fighter were not as fortunate. Nevertheless, top fighters from the United States and Europe were in no shortage during this period.

This period was also characterized by overt racism toward black fighters. Perhaps still reeling from the negativity associated with having the sketchy Jack Johnson as the first prominent black boxer, the boxing establishment locked out many deserving fighters, especially big men like Harry Wills. Jack Dempsey dominated the decade and became boxing's first superhero. Most fight films before Dempsey came around were archaic, often times featuring very little in the way of pleasing action. Fans were awestruck watching the footage of the great 'Manassa Mauler'. He brought a new brutality and savagery into the sport, creating a template of the ideal heavyweight champion. In the process, he became perhaps the biggest celebrity in the land.

The 1920's also saw the beginning of the end for the original 8 weight classes. Title bouts at junior lightweight and junior welterweight began taking place. These divisions were afterthoughts and would be considered so for decades to come, but the blueprint was created.

When looking back, one can begin to notice the shaping of the sport's power structure that still somewhat exists to this day. The promoter became central to the event, an overly visible, meddlesome, and corruptible influence. Tex Rickard, one of the original super-promoters, ruled the sport with an iron fist and began the troubling trend where the major shot-callers in the sport are not objective arbiters, but those with a major financial stake in the actual proceedings of the sport itself.

The problems with not having a singular officiating body like most major sports crystallized during this period. Promoters were in cahoots with sanctioning bodies. Deserving fighters could be ignored for years, as promoters jockeyed to avoid them in order to preserve their meal tickets. Boxing became the only sport (this still exists) where it's all about who you know. In other sports, an athlete could show his skills and advance up the ladder in a manner that was commensurate with his ability. In boxing, a fighter's success would often be tied to his willingness to "play ball" with unscrupulous individuals.

Not that these unpleasant elements didn't exist before, but by the 1920's, one could see some of the negative parts of the sport begin to manifest. The shady side of the business began to take form, with endless boxers fleeced by the sport. Old boxers dying early or losing their mental faculties were rampantly evident. The immense popularity of the professional fight game exposed what a great sport boxing is, but also unveiled some of the things that still cause people to look at it as a dirty business.' [106]

This stereotype of the boxer is what causes George and Candy's scorn when they see Curley's glove.

'The swamper warmed to his gossip. "You seen that glove on his left hand?"

"Yeah. I seen it."

"Well, that glove's fulla vaseline."

"Vaseline? What the hell for?"

---

[106] Unknown, *'1920s Boxing'*, accessed 11/19. https://www.proboxing-fans.com/boxing-101/history/1920s-boxing/

"Well, I tell ya what- Curley says he's keepin' that hand soft for his wife."

George studied the cards absorbedly. "That's a dirty thing to tell around," he said.' [107]

He might be wearing the glove to soothe his callouses after bare knuckle boxing, implying he cares about his wife in bed. It might be a reference to masturbation, or to soft femininity which would be shameful to the tough Curley. The fact Curley is writing off to adverts for dodgy medicine he's seen in the newspaper[108] implies shame, so the implication is he's looking for a form of Viagra and combined with his soft hands, this makes him effeminate. Violence is masculine: it's no wonder why George scoffs when other alternatives are considered.

In the wider world, it's worth noting that Of Mice and Men was written at the time when the Nazi party was gaining power in Germany. The Nazi party also had many supporters in the USA, so Steinbeck, dividing his time between New York and California, may well have seen literal Nazis marching through the streets around him. The biggest rallies were yet to come, however.

'Six and a half months before Adolf Hitler invaded Poland, New York City's Madison Square Garden hosted a rally to celebrate the rise of Nazism in Germany. Inside, more than 20,000 attendees raised Nazi salutes toward a 30-foot-tall portrait of George Washington flanked by swastikas. Outside, police and some 100,000 protestors gathered.

---

[107] Steinbeck, *Of Mice and Men*, 30.

[108] 'Patent Medicine Houses'.

The organization behind the February 20, 1939 event—advertised on the arena's marquee as a "Pro American Rally"—was the German American Bund ("Bund" is German for "federation"). The anti-semitic organization held Nazi summer camps for youth and their families during the 1930s. The Bund's youth members were present that night, as were the Ordnungsdienst, or OD, the group's vigilante police force who dressed in the style of Hitler's SS officers.

Banners at the rally had messages like "Stop Jewish Domination of Christian Americans" and "Wake Up America. Smash Jewish Communism." When the Bund's national leader, Fritz Kuhn, gave his closing speech, he referred to President Franklin Delano Roosevelt as "Rosenfield," and Manhattan District Attorney Thomas Dewey as "Thomas Jewey."

"We, with American ideals, demand that our government shall be returned to the American people who founded it," declared Kuhn, a naturalized American who lost his citizenship during World War II. "If you ask what we are actively fighting for under our charter: First, a socially just, white, Gentile-ruled United States. Second, Gentile-controlled labor unions, free from Jewish Moscow-directed domination."

Kuhn's speech was interrupted by a Jewish-American man named Isadore Greenbaum who charged the stage in protest. Police and the vigilante force quickly tackled him, and proceeded to beat him up on stage. The crowd cheered as they threw him off stage, pulling his pants down in the process. Police charged Greenbaum with disorderly conduct and gave him a $25 fine, about $450 in 2019 dollars.

At the time the rally took place, Hitler was completing his sixth concentration camp; and protesters—many of them Jewish Americans—called attention to the fact that what was happening in Germany could happen in the U.S. "Don't *wait for the concentration camps—Act now!" proclaimed fliers advertising the protest. Outside the rally, people carried signs with messages like "Smash Anti-Semitism" and "Give me a gas mask, I can't stand the smell of Nazis." In some cases, police responded to the protesters with violent attacks. In one instance, a protester escaped a mounted police officer who'd grabbed him by punching his horse in the face. As the rally broke up that night, some protesters were able to slip by police and punch departing Nazis in the face.'* [109]

Of course, sometimes the answer for the reason Steinbeck's books are so violent might be the simplest one. Maybe Steinbeck just liked violent writing. One critic wrote:

'It seems that violence in itself holds an inherent fascination for Steinbeck . . . that it's appeal lies merely in the glitter of the knife, the hangings, shootings, mutilations with which his work is filled.' [110]

Indeed, in his old age, he took pride in the violence of his life. It really was at the heart of his being, as it is in this novella.

'For I have always lived violently, drunk hugely, eaten too much or not at all, slept round the clock or missed two nights of sleeping, worked too hard or too long in glory, or slobbed for a time in utter laziness. I've lifted, pulled chopped, climbed, made love with joy and taken my hangovers as a consequence, not as a punishment.' [111]

---

[109] Unknown, 'Americans hold a Nazi rally in Madison Square Garden', accessed 11/19. https://www.history.com/this-day-in-history/americans-hold-nazi-rally-in-madison-square-garden

[110] Quoted in Parini, *Steinbeck*, 204.

[111] Steinbeck, *Travels with Charley*, 17.

Race and Identity

Of Mice and Men is a key part of the American canon of literature and it is a novel of America at a certain point in history. For British readers, this sense of a single identity might be slightly alien, especially when separated by time. A convenient window into the specifically white American identity of the 1920s inhabited by Steinbeck's characters is through examining some of the rhetoric of the KKK.

Linda Gordon argues that:

'Never an aberration, the KKK might actually have enunciated values with which a majority of 1920s Americans agreed.' [112]

We as readers in the twenty-first century recognise that most, if not all, of what the Ku Klux Klan said and did was violently racist. This was not the case for the average white American outside of the larger cities at the time.

'The Klan was easily at its most popular in the United States during the 1920s, when its reach was nationwide, its members disproportionately middle class, and many of its very visible public activities geared toward festivities, pageants, and social gatherings. In some ways, it was this superficially innocuous Klan that was the most insidious of them all. Packaging its noxious ideology as traditional small-town values and wholesome fun, the Klan of the 1920s encouraged native-born white Americans to believe that bigotry,

---

[112] Gordon, Linda (2017), *The Second Coming of the KKK: The Ku Klux Klan of the 1920s and the American Political Tradition*, New York: Live Right, 36.

intimidation, harassment, and extralegal violence were all perfectly compatible with, if not central to, patriotic respectability.'[113]

Their definition of America was small town and anti-intellectual. The Imperial Wizard[114] Hiram Evans declared:

'We are a movement of the plain people, very weak in matter of culture, intellectual support and trained leadership. We are demanding a return of power into the hands of the everyday, not highly cultured, not overly intellectualised, but not entirely unspoiled and de-americanised average citizen of the old stock.' [115]

The Klan's ideology was a reaction against the modern and progressive 1920s. An American Identity, for this group, was to be specifically white and to have a European heritage.

'Ideologically, the Klan blended xenophobia, religious prejudice, and white supremacy together with a broadly conservative moralism. Amidst a global recession that came in the aftermath of World War I, fear and anxiety were widespread among native-born white Protestants that the country they had known and been accustomed to dominating was coming undone. They worried about an influx of eastern European immigrants who adhered to Communism and other supposedly subversive political creeds, about the seemingly growing influence of Catholics and Jews in American life, and about the migration of African Americans out of the South. The intellectual vogue for religious modernism, the expansion of political and sexual freedoms for women, and the perception that immorality, crime, and vice were

---

[113] Joshua Rothman, 'When Bigotry Paraded Through The Streets', accessed 12/19. https://www.theatlantic.com/politics/archive/2016/12/second-klan/509468/

[114] Leader of the KKK.

[115] Quoted in Gordon, The Return of the KKK, 44.

all on the rise only confirmed the sense that the world was spinning beyond their control.

The Klan advocated the restoration of "true Americanism" and offered members a platform that demonized blacks, Catholics, Jews, Mexicans, Asians, and any other non-white ethnic immigrants while also condemning Communism, most other forms of leftist politics, and "base" cultural influences such as alcohol, birth control, and the teaching of evolution in public schools. Presenting itself in part as a Christian moral reform organization and in part as a vehicle for entrenching the economic and political power of white Anglo-Saxon Protestants, the Klan flourished with the promise that energetic white nationalism and traditional morals would hold back the tides of modernity and ensure that forces scheming to undermine the authority of native-born white Americans would be kept at bay.'[116]

To be American, for many of the smallest communities in 1920s America such as the ranch in which George and Lennie live, meant belonging to a very narrow grouping of people. If you were not part of the white, protestant and long-established American population, popular thought in the 1920 and 1930s held you to be dangerous and therefore deserving of a violent response to any 'wrongdoing'.

For Steinbeck too, it wasn't quite enough just to be born in America to make you an American: it was more of a state of mind. In his old age he decided to sit down and try and summarise his thoughts on what makes someone an American.

'One of the generalities most noted about Americans is that we are a restless, a dissatisfied, a searching people. We brindle and buck under failure, and we

---

[116] Rothman, 'When Bigotry Paraded Through The Streets'.

go mad with dissatisfaction in the face of success. We spend our time searching for security, and hate it when we get it. For the most part we are an intemperate people: we eat too much when we can, drink too much, indulge our senses too much. Even in our so-called vices we are intemperate: a teetotaller is not content not to drink—he must stop all the drinking in the world; a vegetarian among us would outlaw the eating of meat. We work too hard, and many die under the strain; then to make up for that we play with a violence as suicidal' [117]

That excess of hope and then despair, or Eden versus damnation, is what makes this a truly American novel.

██████████████████████████████████ The answer is yes . . . but that 'yes' is not representative of the full picture. The early twentieth century environment in which Steinbeck grew up, and George and Lennie would live, was one where bigotry was mainstream and in white communities it was considered acceptable to hold views that would be repulsive today. Yet Steinbeck decided to include a black character in his 1937 novella who is presented as interesting and intelligent, a relatively unusual decision for a white author of the time period. The inclusion of Crooks, the black stable buck, is an interesting and progressive one, as is Steinbeck's views on race[118]:

'I am constantly amazed by the qualities we expect in Negroes. No race has ever offered another such high regard. We expect Negroes to be wiser than we are, more tolerant than we are, braver, more dignified than we, more self-controlled and self-disciplined. We even demand more talent from then than ourselves. A Negro must be ten times as gifted as a white to receive equal

---

[117] Steinbeck, *America and Americans*, 330.

[118] Published later in 1960, but very much representative of his views at the time of writing.

recognition. We expect Negroes to have more endurance than we in athletics, more courage in defeat, more rhythm and versatility in music and dancing, more controlled emotion in theatre. We expect them to obey rules of conduct that we flout, to be more courteous, more gallant, more proud, more steadfast. In a word, while maintaining that Negroes are inferior to us, by our unquestioning faith in them we prove our conviction that they are superior in many fields, even in fields we are we are presumed to be trained in and they are not.' [119]

The character of Crooks appears to fit with this viewpoint. Crooks reads a dictionary, while the rest of the ranch hands read cowboy magazines. Crooks responds to Curley's Wife with politeness, while George responds to her appearance with insults and rage.

Crooks also seems to be fairly representative of how a black ranch hand could live in real life: segregated and treated slightly disdainfully.

Aaron Barkham was a young boy when the Depression hit. Both he and his father got jobs as miners and their whole family moved into a mining camp. As an older man, he looked back at that time and the families that lived nearby:

'Half the coal camp was coloured. It wasn't anti-coloured. The black people had the same responsibilities as the white. Their lawn was just as green as the white man's. . . Sure, the company tried to play one side agin' [120] *the other. But it didn't work. The coloured and the whites lived side by side. It was somethin' like a checkerboard. There'd be a white family and a coloured family. No sir, there was no racial problem. Yeah, they had a certain feeling*

---

[119] Steinbeck, *America and Americans*, 105.

[120] Against.

about the coloured. They had a certain feelin' about the whites too. Anyone who come into the community had unsatisfactory dealins', if it was coloured or white, he didn't say' [121]

Yet, despite Barkham's memory of a slightly idyllic time, Of Mice and Men was written not especially long after one of the most awful experiences that was researched for this book: the Tulsa Race Massacre.

'By 1921, fueled by oil money, Tulsa was a growing, prosperous city with a population of more than 100,000 people. But crime rates were high, and vigilante justice wasn't uncommon: In August 1920, a white mob took a white teenager accused of murdering a taxi driver from his jail cell at the courthouse and lynched him; newspaper reports claimed the police did little to prevent the lynching.

Tulsa was also a highly segregated city: Most of the city's 10,000 black residents lived in a neighborhood called Greenwood, which included a thriving business district sometimes referred to as the Black Wall Street.

On May 30, 1921, a young black teenager named Dick Rowland entered an elevator at the Drexel Building, an office building on South Main Street. At some point after that, the young white elevator operator, Sarah Page, screamed; Rowland fled the scene. The police were called, and the next morning they arrested Rowland.

By that time, rumors of what supposedly happened on that elevator had circulated through the city's white community. A front-page story in the Tulsa Tribune that afternoon reported that police had arrested Rowland for sexually assaulting Page.

---

[121] Quoted in Terkel, Studs (1970), Hard times: An Oral History of the Great Depression, New York: Pantheon, 205.

As evening fell, an angry white mob was gathering outside the courthouse, demanding the sheriff hand over Rowland. Sheriff Willard McCullough refused, and his men barricaded the top floor to protect the black teenager. Around 9 p.m., a group of about 25 armed black men—including many World War I veterans—went to the courthouse to offer help guarding Rowland. After the sheriff turned them away, some of the white mob tried unsuccessfully to break into the National Guard armory nearby.

With rumors still flying of a possible lynching, a group of around 75 armed blacks returned to the courthouse shortly after 10 pm, where they were met by some 1,500 whites, some of whom also carried weapons.

After shots were fired and chaos broke out, the outnumbered group of blacks retreated to Greenwood.

Over the next several hours, groups of white Tulsans—some of whom were deputized and given weapons by city officials—committed numerous acts of violence against blacks, including shooting an unarmed man in a movie theater.

The false belief that a large-scale insurrection among black Tulsans was underway, including reinforcements from nearby towns and cities with large African-American populations, fueled the growing hysteria.

As dawn broke on June 1, thousands of white citizens poured into the Greenwood District, looting and burning homes and businesses over an area of 35 city blocks. Firefighters who arrived to help put out fires later testified that rioters had threatened them with guns and forced them to leave.

According to a later Red Cross estimate, some 1,256 houses were burned; 215 others were looted but not torched. Two newspapers, a school, a library, a hospital, churches, hotels, stores and many other black-owned businesses were among the buildings destroyed or damaged by fire.

*By the time the National Guard arrived and declared martial law shortly
before noon, the riot had effectively ended. Though guardsmen helped put
out fires, they also imprisoned many black Tulsans, and by June 2 some
6,000 people were under armed guard at the local fairgrounds.'* [122]

This violence was not isolated and lynching was a sadly widespread facet of
race relations in the American South. Take these examples:

*'In June 1920, three black men, circus workers like Elias Clayton, Elmer
Jackson and Isaac McGhie, were lynched in Duluth, Minnesota, accused of
raping a white girl. The alleged victim was later examined by a doctor who
found no evidence of physical assault.*

*Two months later, a mob of over a thousand people stormed a Texas jail and
lynched Lige Daniels, accused of murdering a white woman; photographs of
his dangling body were turned into souvenir postcards. As ever, there were
smirking white crowds below, including children.*

*Later that year, there was another triple lynching in Santa Rosa, California, in
front of spectators, one of whom offered 'vivid' eyewitness account of the
'sickening' event to the press.*

*It was observed at the time that the excuses offered for lynching had grown
ever thinner, and if mobs could no longer be bothered to rationalise torture
and murder. Once the only 'adequate provocation' acknowledged by public
opinion was the 'ravishment of a white woman by a Negro', noted the Dallas
Express. Now 'public opinion has become more indulgent. Among the
'reasons' offered for the summary execution of black Americans in the early*

---

122 Unknown, *'Tulsa Race Massacre'*, accessed 11/19. https://www.history.com/topics/roaring-twenties/tulsa-race-massacre

years of the twentieth century were 'wild talk', 'gambling dispute', 'wage dispute', 'debt dispute' and 'circulating literature'.' [123]

Could Crooks face lynching? Curley's wife certainly thought so.

'She turned on him in scorn. "Listen, Nigger," she said. "You know what I can do to you if you open your trap?"
Crooks stared hopelessly at her, and then he sat down on his bunk and drew into himself.

She closed on him. "You know what I could do?"

Crooks seemed to grow smaller, and he pressed himself against the wall. "Yes, ma'am."

"Well, you keep your place then, Nigger. I could get you strung up on a tree so easy it ain't even funny."'

It was also entirely legal for someone to lynch Crooks if they wanted to. Horrifically, a loophole existed where the crime of lynching was legal[124] until disturbingly recently. Many attempts had been taken to ban it, but these all failed.

'In December 2018, the U.S. Senate passed a federal anti-lynching bill for the first time. The significant milestone is preceded by at least 240 failed attempts since 1901 to pass any bill or resolution mentioning lynching in Congress. These attempts to outlaw lynching peaked during Franklin D. Roosevelt's presidency…

---

[123] Churchwell, *Behold America*, 95.

[124] If a black person was lynched, the culprits would be charged murder, not specifically lynching.

In the mid-30s, the NAACP[125] persuaded Democratic Senators Robert Wagner and Edward Costigan to sponsor an anti-lynching bill. The legislation couldn't survive without the president's support, so Eleanor arranged a meeting with White and FDR to try to convince the president to endorse it. The meeting diddn't go well.

"Somebody's been priming you. Was it my wife?" FDR asked in annoyance after White presented his case. "If I come out for the anti-lynching bill now, [southern Democrats] will block every bill I ask Congress to pass to keep America from collapsing. I just can't take the risk."

Those bills he wanted to pass to keep America from collapsing were part of the New Deal. At the time, "the southern Democrats in the Senate are holding the New Deal hostage and refusing to move on New Deal issues unless the rest of the Democratic party backs off the anti-lynching bills," says Eric Rauchway, a history professor at the University of California, Davis...

Instead, FDR never gave his support, and the anti-lynching bills introduced during his term were "filibustered [126] to death," Rauchway says. Senator Richard Russell, for whom one of the three Senate office buildings is still named, filibustered a 1935 anti-lynching bill for six days in order to kill it (three decades later, he also filibustered the 1964 civil rights bill). In 1937, Eleanor sat in the Senate Gallery for days as Senators filibustered another anti-lynching bill to death. Even in the early '40s, southern Democratic

---

[125] North American Association of Coloured People, who stood up for the rights of non-white people.

[126] This is when a member of a legislative body blocks a law or motion passing but doesn't technically break any rules. The most common way to do this is to keep talking for so long that the legislative body misses the deadline, or to talk for so long everyone else just wants the person to shut up so they vote their way.

senators threatened not to support World War II bills unless their colleagues dropped anti-lynching legislation.

The NAACP estimates that between 1882 and 1968, 4,743 lynchings occurred in the U.S., and that the majority of the people killed in these lynchings were black. Members of Congress continued to sponsor anti-lynching legislation after FDR's death in 1945, and Franklin D. Roosevelt, Jr. actually tried to pass anti-lynching laws several times in the '50s. But none made it through the Senate until Kamala Harris, Cory Booker and Tim Scott sponsored an anti-lynching bill as the only black members of the 2018 Senate (it still needs to pass in the House and receive a presidential signature before it becomes law).

Before that recent bill, the last time Congress introduced anti-lynching legislation was in the mid-1960s, around the time that Democratic President Lyndon B. Johnson signed the Civil Rights Act.' [127]

However, even though black people were the primary target of violence across much, if not all of the American South, the Mexican community was the target for economically motivated hate. This is not a widely recognised episode in the narrative of American race relations, and deserves recognition here. Crooks' fears were real, but any community hate in the Salinas Valley could well have been turned towards the Mexican community.

'Americans are largely unaware that Mexicans were frequently the targets of lynch mobs, from the mid-19th century until well into the 20th century, second only to African-Americans in the scale and scope of the crimes. One case, largely overlooked or ignored by American journalists but not by the Mexican

---

[127] Becky Little, *'Why FDR Didn't Support Eleanor Roosevelt's Anti-Lynching Campaign'*, accessed 11/19. https://www.history.com/news/fdr-eleanor-roosevelt-anti-lynching-bill

government, was that of seven Mexican shepherds hanged by white vigilantes near Corpus Christi, Tex., in late November 1873. The mob was probably trying to intimidate the shepherds' employer into selling his land. None of the killers were arrested.

From 1848 to 1928, mobs murdered thousands of Mexicans, though surviving records allowed us to clearly document only about 547 cases. These lynchings occurred not only in the southwestern states of Arizona, California, New Mexico and Texas, but also in states far from the border, like Nebraska and Wyoming.

Some of these cases did appear in press accounts, when reporters depicted them as violent public spectacles, as they did with many lynchings of African-Americans in the South. For example, on July 5, 1851, a mob of 2,000 in Downieville, Calif., watched the extralegal hanging of a Mexican woman named Juana Loaiza, who had been accused of having murdered a white man named Frank Cannon.

Such episodes were not isolated to the turbulent gold rush period. More than a half-century later, on Nov. 3, 1910, a mob snatched a 20-year-old Mexican laborer, Antonio Rodríguez, from a jail in Rock Springs, Tex. The authorities had arrested him on charges that he had killed a rancher's wife. Mob leaders bound him to a mesquite tree, doused him with kerosene and burned him alive. The El Paso Herald reported that thousands turned out to witness the event; we found no evidence that anyone was ever arrested.

While there were similarities between the lynchings of blacks and Mexicans, there were also clear differences. One was that local authorities and deputized citizens played particularly conspicuous roles in mob violence against Mexicans.

99

On Jan. 28, 1918, a band of Texas Rangers and ranchers arrived in the village of Porvenir in Presidio County, Tex. Mexican outlaws had recently attacked a nearby ranch, and the posse presumed that the locals were acting as spies and informants for Mexican raiders on the other side of the border. The group rounded up nearly two dozen men, searched their houses, and marched 15 of them to a rock bluff near the village and executed them. The Porvenir massacre, as it has become known, was the climactic event in what Mexican-Americans remember as the Hora de Sangre (Hour of Blood). It led, the following year, to an investigation by the Texas Legislature and reform of the Rangers.

Between 1915 and 1918, vigilantes, local law officers and Texas Rangers executed, without due process, unknown thousands of Mexicans for their alleged role in a revolutionary uprising known as the Plan de San Diego. White fears of Mexican revolutionary violence exploded in July and August 1915, after Mexican raiders committed a series of assaults on the economic infrastructure of the Lower Rio Grande Valley in resistance to white dominance. The raids unleashed a bloody wave of retaliatory action amid a climate of intense paranoia.

While there are certainly instances in the history of the American South where law officers colluded in mob action, the level of engagement by local and state authorities in the reaction to the Plan de San Diego was remarkable. The lynchings persisted into the 1920s, eventually declining largely because of pressure from the Mexican government.

Historians have often ascribed to the South a distinctiveness that has set it apart from the rest of the United States. In so doing, they have created the impression of a peculiarly benighted region plagued by unparalleled levels of racial violence. The story of mob violence against Mexicans in the Southwest compels us to rethink the history of lynching.

Southern blacks were the group most often targeted, but comparing the histories of the South and the West strengthens our understanding of mob violence in both.' [128]

The threat of lynching against Crooks was very real, and others like him had been killed for less than being in a room with a white woman. Yet depending on the whims of a mob, a Mexican farmer, or Lennie after being accused of assault, or George for being rude to Curley's Wife, could also have faced this same injustice.

[128] William D. Carrigan and Clive Webb, 'When Americans Lynched Mexicans', accessed 11/19. https://www.nytimes.com/2015/02/20/opinion/when-americans-lynched-mexicans.html

A Woman's Place

Steinbeck's relationship with women was complex to say the least, and this needs to be discussed in order to understand the character of Curley's wife in her proper context.

He never got on with his mother, feeling that she was not supportive of his career. His sister recalled:

"'John had complicated relations with Mother'" [129]

Ultimately, they never reconciled, even on her deathbed.

'It was not simply that he felt she had never given him the unconditional love a child must have; she had, in fact loved him very much. Her obsessive concern for his education and moral development was, in part, an expression of love. But it was always a contingent love, which meant that her son never felt satisfied; whatever he accomplished he could never really measure up in the way she would have liked. Something was missing.' [130]

While accusations fly that Steinbeck was an abuser of women, only one can be definitively proved. While single after university, Steinbeck committed an assault against a woman, Polly, who he was dating.

'Polly had no interest in keeping up with Steinbeck, who was soon terribly drunk; several hours later, after making a pass which Polly rebuffed, he

_____

[129] Quoted in Parini, *Steinbeck*, 171.

[130] Parini, *Steinbeck,* 171.

seems to have gone crazy. He began screaming at her, then dragged her to the top floor of the house and dangled her by the ankles from the second storey window. Polly shrieked for help, begging him to bring her back into the room, and were it not for the intervention of Lloyd Shebley [his neighbour], Polly might easily have been killed. One can hardly overestimated the insanity of this particular act.' [131]

Luckily Polly was not physically hurt. Steinbeck was not charged with any crime and the police were not involved. The summer he met Polly he also met Carol and followed her to San Francisco after she moved house. They would later get married. She supported his work financially and emotionally. She was his spouse at the time of the writing of Of Mice and Men, but their marriage eventually fractured.

'Years after his divorce from Carol, Steinbeck advised another writer that "your work is your only weapon.". . . John and Carol's collaboration in Steinbeck's signature work of the 1930s—always his work, rarely hers—was their mutual weapon against poverty and insecurity until fortune and fame— his, not hers—intervened. The title of Steinbeck's anthem of the Great Depression, The Grapes of Wrath, was her idea. The progressive politics of the protest novels that preceded it—In Dubious Battle and Of Mice and Men —were hers before they were his. She became his muse and motivator, typist and editor, connector and companion. But the 12-year experience drained and disoriented her, leaving her ill-equipped to cope with wealth, notoriety, and competition from the woman who became Steinbeck's second wife in 1943.' [132]

---

[131] Parini, Steinbeck, 98.

[132] William Ray, 'Susan Shillinglaw Details John Steinbeck's Dramatic Marriage to Carol Henning', accessed 11/19. http://www.steinbecknow.com/2013/10/12/susan-shillinglaw-details-john-steinbecks-dramatic-marriage-to-carol-henning/

Steinbeck did not treat Carol well, to say the least.

'Indeed, Steinbeck must be castigated for his treatment of Carol, which borders on gross inhumanity. He seems not to have appreciated the massive efforts she made on his behalf: the sacrifices, the endless adjustments to meet his schedule, the willingness to type manuscripts on demand, the self-repression.' [133]

He met the beautiful Gwyn when she was a nightclub singer and he was separated from Carol. They had two sons together, but again, this marriage broke up. After Steinbeck's death, Gwyn (by then Gwyn Conger-Steinbeck) gave interviews about her alleged[134] mistreatment during her marriage. These cast his views on women in a new light.

'Conger Steinbeck described a husband who was emotionally distant and demanding. "Like so many writers, he had several lives, and in each he was spoilt, and in each he felt he was king," she wrote. "From the time John awoke to the time he went to bed, I had to be his slave."

Conger Steinbeck first met the author as a nightclub singer in 1938, when he was married to his first wife, Carol Henning. In 1941, Conger Steinbeck alleges that the author sat her down with Henning and told them both: "Whichever of you ladies needs me the most and wants me the most, then that's the woman I'm going to have."

---

[133] David Lister, *'Steinbeck: not so saintly: He was a spoilt rich kid who mistreated his wife. David Lister looks at a new biography of the author'*, accessed 11/19. https://www.independent.co.uk/news/uk/home-news/steinbeck-not-so-saintly-he-was-a-spoilt-rich-kid-who-mistreated-his-wife-david-lister-looks-at-a-1431995.html

[134] Their divorce was incredibly messy, and some statements were made on both sides that were later proven to be false. This claim is not one specific to their divorce, but the proceedings during their separation make a lot of the statements against Steinbeck worth checking.

Describing their wedding night, Conger Steinbeck recalls one "Lady M"
ringing their bedroom and speaking to the author for more than an hour on
the phone. Conger Steinbeck alludes to Lady M being his mistress, writing
that the pair had a "matinee about three times a week".' [135]

Later in life Steinbeck met and married his last wife, Elaine, a successful
Broadway director in her own right.

'Mrs. Steinbeck met John Steinbeck during a visit to California in 1950. Mr.
Steinbeck had been asked to escort Ava Gardner to a dinner party in Carmel
and when Miss Gardner was unable to attend, the hostess asked to pick up
the actress Ann Sothern and "a friend." The friend was Elaine Anderson
Scott. They were married that same year, and until his death, Mr. Steinbeck
would often raise a glass at parties and offer a toast to Ava Gardner.' [136]

She remembers him fondly.

'I spent his last 20 years with him and he was the best company I've ever
been with. . . He was very funny, had a marvellous mind and was a wonderful
companion.' [137]

Despite his many, many flaws as a romantic partner, Steinbeck seemed to get
it right in the end.

---

[135] Sian Cain, *'John Steinbeck was a sadistic womaniser, says wife in memoir'*, accessed 10/19. https://www.theguardian.com/books/2018/sep/07/john-steinbeck-a-sadistic-womaniser-says-wife-in-memoir

[136] Enid Nemy, *'Elaine Steinbeck, 88, Author's widow, dies'*, accessed 11/19. https://www.nytimes.com/2003/04/29/books/elaine-steinbeck-88-author-s-widow-dies.html

[137] David Lister, *'Steinbeck: Not So Saintly'*.

As mentioned before, sometimes a writer fully explains what they meant by a character, as Steinbeck did in a letter to a nervous actress when Of Mice and Men opened as a play.

'Dear Miss Luce:
Annie Laurie says you are worried about your playing of the part of Curley's wife although from the reviews it appears that you are playing it marvelously. I am deeply grateful to you and to the others in the cast for your feeling about the play. You have surely made it much more than it was by such a feeling.

About the girl—I don't know of course what you think about her, but perhaps if I should tell you a little about her as I know her, it might clear your feeling about her.

She grew up in an atmosphere of fighting and suspicion. Quite early she learned that she must never trust anyone but she was never able to carry out what she learned. A natural trustfulness broke through constantly and every time it did, she got her. Her moral training was most rigid. She was told over and over that she must remain a virgin because that was the only way she could get a husband. This was harped on so often that it became a fixation. It would have been impossible to seduce her. She had only that one thing to sell and she knew it.

Now, she was trained by threat not only at home but by other kids. And any show of fear or weakness brought an instant persecution. She learned to be hard to cover her fright. And automatically she became hardest when she was most frightened. She is a nice, kind girl, not a floozy. No man has ever considered her as anything except a girl to try to make. She has never talked to a man except in the sexual fencing conversation. She is not highly sexed particularly but knows instinctively that if she is to be noticed at all, it will be because some one finds her sexually desirable.

As to her actual sexual life—she has had none except with Curley and there has probably been no consummation there since Curley would not consider her gratification and would probably be suspicious if she had any. Consequently she is a little starved. She knows utterly nothing about sex except the mass misinformation girls tell one another. If anyone—a man or woman—ever gave her a break—treated her like a person—she would be a slave to that person. Her craving for contact is immense but she, with her background, is incapable of conceiving any contact without some sexual context. With all this—if you knew her, if you could ever break down a thousand little defences she has built up, you would find a nice person, an honest person, and you would end up by loving her. But such a thing could never happen.

I hope you won't think I'm preaching. I've known this girl and I'm just trying to tell you what she is like. She is afraid of everyone in the world. You've known girls like that, haven't you? You can see them in Central Park on a hot night. They travel in groups for protection. They pretend to be wise and hard and voluptuous.

I have a feeling that you know all this and that you are doing all this. Please forgive me if I seem to intrude on your job. I don't intend to and I am only writing this because Annie Laurie said you wondered about the girl. It's a devil of a hard part. I am very happy that you have it.

Sincerely,

John Steinbeck'

As Steinbeck has mentioned sex in this letter, but never explicitly in his book[138], it bears mentioning here. She is presented as provocative, and may well have been relatively informed compared to previous generations.

'Closely associated with the rise of the flapper, the twenties gave rise to a frank, national discussion about sex. But this trend, too, had been building over time. As early as 1913, the Atlantic Monthly announced that the clock had tolled "Sex o'clock in America," indicating a "Repeal of Reticence" about issues that had once been considered taboo. To be sure, these trends accelerated after World War I: surveys suggest that 14 percent of women born before 1900 engaged in pre-marital sex by the age of 25, while as many as 39 percent of women who came of age in the 1910s and 1920s lost their virginity before marriage.' [139]

The fact she decided to marry Curley, before or after sleeping with him, is in itself a little surprising, considering:

'The marriage rate in the United States fell a staggering 22 percent between the years of 1929 to 1933.' [140]

However, despite a mild flirtation with Lennie and Slim, was she a 'good' wife? In 1939, doctors designed a 'scientific' marriage test to see how strong a relationship was. Aside from obvious signs of weakness like adultery:

---

[138] Despite the fact that whenever this book is taught in a classroom, at least one student will shout 'CURLEY'S WIFE IS A SLUT'.

[139] Joshua Zeitz, *'Age of Convergence'*, accessed 11/19. https://ap.gilderlehrman.org/essays/roaring-twenties

[140] Brittany Brolley, *'How marriages have changed over the last 100 years'*, accessed 11/19. https://www.thelist.com/132979/how-marriages-have-changed-over-the-last-100-years/

'wearing red nail polish and going to bed while wearing curlers are also considered marital vices.' [141]

Compare this advice to Curley's wife's first appearance:

'Both men glanced up, for the rectangle of sunshine in the doorway was cut off. A girl was standing there looking in. She had full, rouged lips and wide-spaced eyes, heavily made up. Her fingernails were red. Her hair hung in little rolled clusters, like sausages. She wore a cotton house dress and red mules, on the insteps of which were little bouquets of red ostrich feathers. "I'm lookin' for Curley," she said. Her voice had a nasal, brittle quality.' [142]

Her appearance signifies, very strongly, that she is not a good wife.

Why exactly was Curley's wife hanging around the farm all the time? Her entrances and exits in the novella just seem to display boredom and a need for attention. Again, the answer of 'women didn't work in those days' isn't quite full enough: She may well have been forced into this lifestyle due to legislation designed to protect male employment.

'In 1930, the United States needed a miracle. Months before, the stock market had crashed, and the economy had begun to tank with it. As the Great Depression pummeled millions of American workers, Frances Perkins, New York's Commissioner of Labor, warned that New York faced a particular threat from a surprising group: Married women with jobs.

---

[141] Matthew Moore, *'Mark your wives: The 1930s marriage test'*, accessed 11/19. https://www.telegraph.co.uk/news/newstopics/howaboutthat/1954587/Mark-your-wives-The-1930s-marriage-test.html

[142] Steinbeck, *Of Mice and Men*, 34.

"The woman 'pin-money worker' who competes with the necessity worker is a menace to society, a selfish, shortsighted creature, who ought to be ashamed of herself," Perkins said. "Until we have every woman in this community earning a living wage...I am not willing to encourage those who are under no economic necessities to compete with their charm and education, their superior advantages, against the working girl who has only her two hands."

Within two years, Perkins would go on to become Secretary of Labor in President Franklin D. Roosevelt's cabinet. And though she is known as one of the architects of the New Deal, her attitudes toward working women were shared by many who embraced FDR's seemingly liberal economic policies of relief for unemployed workers.

Perkins wasn't the only one who was suspicious of married women in the workplace. The 1930s would see a spike in policies and laws that discriminated against, even forbade, women to work when they were married. During the Great Depression, discrimination against their employment even became law.

"Nine states had marriage [work ban] laws prior to the Depression," writes historian historian Megan McDonald Way, "and by 1940, 26 states restricted married women's employment in state government jobs." As women around the country struggled to make ends meet during the nation's deepest economic crisis, they became an easy scapegoat for people looking for someone to blame.

By the time Perkins made her speech, the debate over working women—and whether women should work once they married—had been raging for decades. Arguments about married women's work often centered on the idea of "pin money." Originally coined to refer to the small amounts of money women spent on fancy items, it had become shorthand for all women's work by the 20th century.

"The revised idea of pin money," writes Janice Traflet, "increasingly served as a justification for paying women (including working-class women) lower wages than men." Women's work, and their expenditures, were cast as inconsequential and foolish, Traflet writes, yet in competition with the ability of men to earn money to support their families.

Family support became more important than ever after the Stock Market Crash of 1929. Shortly after Perkins delivered her speech in 1930, U.S. unemployment hit a rate of 25 percent nationally—and the question of whether married women should hold jobs became even more controversial.

In fact, businesses had been banning married women from work since at least the 1880s. Marriage bars were designed not only to reserve employment opportunities for men, but to ensure that unmarried women without families to support were kept in the lowest paying, least prestigious positions. Single women most commonly held clerical and teaching jobs, both of which had come to be seen as "women's work" by the 1930s. (Black women were subject to fewer marriage bars, but had little access to the jobs available to white, middle-class women at the time.)

In today's era of relatively strong workplace discrimination laws, the prevalence of marriage bars can seem astonishing. As Way notes, marriage bars were common throughout the insurance, publishing, and banking industries, and imposed with abandon by private firms in other white-collar professions. The laws and policies reflected common misconceptions about working women. It was assumed that women might work outside the home before marriage, but that they would want to return to the home sphere once

111

they wed. Those middle-class married women who did seek employment during the Depression were often met with hostility.

The arguments against married women working were personal. In Wisconsin, for example, lawmakers passed a resolution in 1935 stating that when married women with working husbands got jobs, they became the "calling card for disintegration of family life." The committee added that "The large number of husbands and wives working for the state raises a serious moral question, as this committee feels that the practice of birth control is encouraged, and the selfishness that arises from the income of employment of husband and wife bids fair to break down civilization and a healthy atmosphere."

In 1932, the federal government even got involved in marriage bars. Section 213 of the Economy Act of 1932 included a section that required the government to fire one member of each married couple working in government. Since women's jobs inevitably paid less than men's, they largely paid the price.

In order to prevent women from going by other names to sidestep losing their jobs, the federal government also began requiring women with federal jobs to use their husbands' names in 1933. Some women even went as far as marrying men without federal jobs without telling anyone so that they wouldn't be fired when their coworkers learned of their wedding. Though women's groups and individual women who were banned from federal service rigorously protested the rule, it would stay in place for the rest of the Great Depression.

Ironically, married women managed to make inroads into the labor market despite the discrimination they faced during the Great Depression. As historian Winifred D. Wandersee Bolin notes, the number of married women workers grew between 1920 and 1940. "The gains of the 1930s were not nearly as dramatic as those of earlier decades," she wrote. "What is significant is that they were made at a time of great economic stagnation—at a time when women were under a great deal of public pressure to leave the labor market in order to avoid competing with men for the short supply of jobs."

Section 213 stayed in force for five years until it was repealed after intensive lobbying by women's groups in 1937. The repeal represented a victory for its opponents. But the damage was already done: As the New York Times reported at the time, only 154 out of about 1,600 government workers who lost their jobs—most women—got their jobs back. And anti-woman attitudes persisted through the end of the Depression.

In 1936, only 15 percent of respondents to a poll in Fortune Magazine asking "Do you believe that women should have a full-time job outside the home?" answered yes. "Simply fire the women who shouldn't be working anyway, and hire the men," wrote journalist Norman Cousins in 1939. "Presto! No unemployment. No relief rolls. No depression." His facetious words reflected how controversial working women were even after Section 213's repeal.

The idea of white, middle-class married women working didn't really become socially acceptable until the 1940s, when World War II opened up a large number of essential war jobs for women. State bars and policies against married and working women were repealed around that time due to a shortage of male labor as men went to war. Women's work threatened men *who had long held economic power—until the nation's power was threatened by absent men.'* [143]

Of course, with most (if not all) school texts, there is a link back to the Bible, and Curley's wife falls within that.

'[His books include] almost to the point of misogyny, the fallen woman. . . it follows that the women will often get the blame for Eden's problems as feminist critics have often pointed out' [144]

Just like in the story of Adam and Eve, it is the woman's fault that the men will never get back into Eden and get their dream.

There might have been a model for Curley's wife based on a woman Steinbeck dated during his youth called Mary Ardath, who he met when she was a waitress at his favourite Italian restaurant. She certainly served as the model for other 'fallen woman' characters, though she seems quite fun as a person based on how she is described.

'Ardath was a beautiful if rather unsophisticated woman: slender-hipped, green-eyed, with blonde hair she pulled back and tied with a ribbon. She was also ambitious, and the idea of marriage to a down-and-out reporter and would-be novelist did not appeal to her.' [145]

In the end, he dumped her when she didn't live up to his preconceived notions about his ideal woman. She loved show-tunes, he loved classical

[143] Erin Blakemore, *'Why Many Married Women Were Banned From Working During the Great Depression'*, accessed 11/19. https://www.history.com/news/great-depression-married-women-employment

[144] Parimi, *Steinbeck*, 167.

[145] Parini, *Steinbeck*, 75.

music. She enjoyed dancing, he enjoyed moping and writing. Even though it was probably his fault since he objectified this girl rather than get to know her, this was the germ of the disappointing woman who didn't meet her potential that appears as a trope in so many of his books.

Conclusion

I went for lunch with a friend on a rainy October day and mentioned that I was writing this book.

"Oh." She said.

"How are you going to write about the glove full of Vaseline?"

This friend works in The City and had not even thought about Of Mice and Men since her teenage years, and yet she remembered a relatively minor quotation. The teaching, and re-teaching, and under-teaching, and over-teaching, of this novella have rendered it a part of most UK adults' memories of school.

I'd taught it nine times[146] before sitting down to write this book and felt like I knew it well, but upon the slightest bit of research I realised most of what I had spouted in class was reductive and clichéd. I deliberately set out to avoid any mentions of 'the main themes' that have been recounted so many times as to fully remove this novella from any meaning for young people.

At the most literal level, we can all relate to wanting something that may never happen. I dream of a house with a library like Belle's in Beauty and the Beast, and travelling the world with my partner, and taking this series into the bestseller lists. We've all made a mistake, albeit not to the level of killing your boss' daughter-in-law. But, more than that, we're all reacting to the hidden ethereal cues of the landscape around us, and we've all been struck by the majesty of a view in the same way Steinbeck was by the Salinas Valley.

---

[146] And twice more during the writing.

If you don't think it's relevant for today, then check Bruce Springsteen's song 'The Ghost of Tom Joad', based on Steinbeck's The Grapes of Wrath. Springsteen summarised Steinbeck perfectly, reflecting how I feel upon writing this book.

'There's always something being revealed—about them, about you. That's always exciting. Even if the stuff is dark, even if there's tragedy involved, it's still exciting. The truth is always hopeful. It's always inspiring, no matter what it is.' [147]

[147] Gary Graff, *'The stories behind the songs: The Ghost Of Tom Joad by Bruce Springsteen'*, accessed 10/19. https://www.loudersound.com/features/the-stories-behind-the-songs-the-ghost-of-tom-joad-by-bruce-springsteen

Bibliography

Samuel J Abrams, *'The American Dream is Alive and Well'*, accessed 10/19. https://www.nytimes.com/2019/02/05/opinion/american-dream.html? module=inline

Kimberley Amadeo, *'What is the American Dream? The History that made it possible'*, accessed 10/19. https://www.thebalance.com/what-is-the-american-dream-quotes-and-history-3306009

Benson, Jackson J (ed, 1990), *The Short Novels of John Steinbeck*, USA: Duke University Press

The Bible (New International Version), *'Genesis 4'*, accessed 10/19. https://www.biblegateway.com/passage/?search=Genesis+4&version=NIV

Erin Blakemore, *'Why Many Married Women Were Banned From Working During the Great Depression'*, accessed 11/19. https://www.history.com/news/ great-depression-married-women-employment

Victoria Brignell, *'When the Disabled were Segregated'*, accessed 11/19. https://www.newstatesman.com/society/2010/12/disabled-children-british

Brittany Brolley, *'How marriages have changed over the last 100 years'*, accessed 11/19. https://www.thelist.com/132979/how-marriages-have-changed-over-the-last-100-years/

Robert Burns, *'To A Mouse'*, accessed 10/19. http://www.robertburns.org.uk/ Assets/Poems_Songs/toamouse.htm

Linda Cameron, 'Agricultural Depression, 1920–1934', accessed 11/19. https://www.mnopedia.org/agricultural-depression-1920-1934

Sian Cain, 'John Steinbeck was a sadistic womaniser, says wife in memoir', accessed 10/19. https://www.theguardian.com/books/2018/sep/07/john-steinbeck-a-sadistic-womaniser-says-wife-in-memoir

Sarah Churchwell, 'End of the American dream? The dark history of 'America first'', accessed 11/19. https://www.theguardian.com/books/2018/apr/21/end-of-the-american-dream-the-dark-history-of-america-first

Churchwell, Sarah (2018), Behold America: A History of America First and The American Dream, UK: Bloomsbury.

Egan, Timothy (2006), The Worst Hard Time: The Untold Story of Those Who Survived The Great American Dustbowl, New York: Houghton Mifflin Harcourt.

Lyn Gardner, 'Of Mice and Men: Birmingham Rep', accessed 11/19. https://www.theguardian.com/stage/2001/nov/17/theatre.artsfeatures1

Gordon, Linda (2017), The Second Coming of the KKK: The Ku Klux Klan of the 1920s and the American Political Tradition, New York: Live Right.

Gary Graff, 'The stories behind the songs: The Ghost Of Tom Joad by Bruce Springsteen', accessed 10/19. https://www.loudersound.com/features/the-stories-behind-the-songs-the-ghost-of-tom-joad-by-bruce-springsteen

Carol Graham, 'Is The American Dream Really Dead?', accessed 10/19. https://www.theguardian.com/inequality/2017/jun/20/is-the-american-dream-really-dead

Guthrie, Woodie (2004 ed), *Bound for Glory*, UK: Penguin.

Woody Guthrie, *'Do Re Mi'*, accessed 10/19. https://genius.com/Woody-guthrie-do-re-mi-lyrics

Brian Hoey, *'Nine Fascinating Facts About John Steinbeck's Of Mice and Men'*, accessed 11/19. https://blog.bookstellyouwhy.com/nine-fascinating-facts-about-john-steinbecks-of-mice-and-men

LEAP, *'History of Disability Rights'*, accessed 11/19. https://www.leapinfo.org/advocacy/history-of-disability-rights/1930s

Becky Little, *'Why FDR Didn't Support Eleanor Roosevelt's Anti-Lynching Campaign'*, accessed 11/19. https://www.history.com/news/fdr-eleanor-roosevelt-anti-lynching-bill

David Lister, *'Steinbeck: not so saintly: He was a spoilt rich kid who mistreated his wife. David Lister looks at a new biography of the author'*, accessed 11/19. https://www.independent.co.uk/news/uk/home-news/steinbeck-not-so-saintly-he-was-a-spoilt-rich-kid-who-mistreated-his-wife-david-lister-looks-at-a-1431995.html

Thomas Malory, *'Le Morte D'Arthur'*, accessed 10/19. https://www.gutenberg.org/files/1251/1251-h/1251-h.htm.

Catherine McNichol Stock, *'Violence in the 1930s'*, accessed 11/19. https://www.nytimes.com/roomfordebate/2011/01/10/assassins-and-american-history/violence-in-the-1930s

Miller, Nathan (2003), *New World Coming: The 1920s and the Making of Modern America*, US: Da Capo Press.

Matthew Moore, *'Mark your wives: The 1930s marriage test'*, accessed 11/19. https://www.telegraph.co.uk/news/newstopics/howaboutthat/1954587/Mark-your-wives-The-1930s-marriage-test.html

Amy Nicholson, *'Mary Pickford: The Woman Who Shaped Hollywood'*, accessed 11/19. http://www.bbc.com/culture/story/20190204-mary-pickford-the-woman-who-shaped-hollywood

Parini, Jay (1994), *John Steinbeck, A Biography*, UK: Heinemann

Jayne Anne Phillips, *'True Crime: America's Most Notorious Ladykiller'*, accessed 11/19. https://www.telegraph.co.uk/culture/books/10816712/True-crime-Americas-most-notorious-ladykiller.html

John J Raskob, *'Everybody Ought To Be Rich'*, accessed 11/19. https://www.joshuakennon.com/wp-content/uploads/2013/01/Everybody-Ought-to-Be-Rich.pdf

Neil Rathnell, *'When is a Play not a Play?'*, accessed 10/19. https://neilrathmell.com/2016/02/03/when-is-a-play-not-a-play/

William Ray, *'Susan Shillinglaw Details John Steinbeck's Dramatic Marriage to Carol Henning'*, accessed 11/19. http://www.steinbecknow.com/2013/10/12/susan-shillinglaw-details-john-steinbecks-dramatic-marriage-to-carol-henning/

William Ray, *'Why did George Orwell name Steinbeck a Communist?'*, accessed 11/19. http://www.steinbecknow.com/2013/09/19/george-orwell-steinbeck-communist/

Franklin D Roosevelt, *'Second Bill of Rights Speech'*, accessed 11/19. https://www.nesri.org/resources/second-bill-of-rights-speech-by-franklin-d-roosevelt

Joshua Rothman, *'When Bigotry Paraded Through The Streets'*, accessed 12/19. https://www.theatlantic.com/politics/archive/2016/12/second-klan/509468/

Marcia Salazar, *'John Steinbeck's Phalanx Theory'*, accessed 11/19. https://periodicos.ufsc.br/index.php/desterro/article/viewFile/8798/9820..

Joe Sommerlad, *'Karl Marx at 200: Ten Left Wing writers following in the footsteps of a giant'*, accessed 11/19. https://www.independent.co.uk/arts-entertainment/books/features/karl-marx-200-years-anniversary-left-wing-novelists-george-orwell-hg-wells-john-steinbeck-a8333991.html

Steinbeck, John (2003), *America and Americans,* USA: Viking Penguin.

John Steinbeck, *'Miss Luce Letter'*, accessed 10/19. https://jwpblog.files.wordpress.com/2017/09/letter-to-claire-luce.doc

John Steinbeck, *'Nobel Prize Acceptance Speech'*, accessed 11/19. https://www.nobelprize.org/prizes/literature/1962/steinbeck/25229-john-steinbeck-banquet-speech-1962/

Steinbeck, John (2006 ed), *Of Mice and Men*, UK: Penguin

Steinbeck, John (2017 ed), *The Grapes of Wrath*, UK: Penguin.

John Steinbeck, *'The Harvest Gypsies'* (excerpt), accessed 11/19. https:// www.commonlit.org/en/texts/excerpt-from-the-harvest-gypsies

Steinbeck, John (1997 ed), *Travels with Charley*, UK: Penguin.

Studs Terkel, *'Firsthand Accounts of the Great Depression'*, accessed 11/19. https://www.facinghistory.org/mockingbird/firsthand-accounts-great-depression

Terkel, Studs (1970), *Hard times: An Oral History of the Great Depression,* New York: Pantheon.

Ashley Turner, *'Mike Pence says the American dream was 'dying' before Trump became president'*, accessed 11/19. https://www.cnbc.com/ 2019/04/11/mike-pence-says-the-american-dream-was-dying-until-trump-was-inaugurated.html

Unknown, *'1920s Boxing'*, accessed 11/19. https://www.proboxing-fans.com/ boxing-101/history/1920s-boxing/

Unknown, *'Five Fascinating Facts about Of Mice and Men'*, accessed 11/19. https://interestingliterature.com/2015/10/07/five-fascinating-facts-about-of-mice-and-men/

Unknown, *'New Deal'*, accessed 11/19. https://www.history.com/topics/great-depression/new-deal

Unknown, *'Americans hold a Nazi rally in Madison Square Garden'*, accessed 11/19. https://www.history.com/this-day-in-history/americans-hold-nazi-rally-in-madison-square-garden

Unknown, *'Tulsa Race Massacre'*, accessed 11/19. https://www.history.com/topics/roaring-twenties/tulsa-race-massacre

Watkins, T H (1993), *The Great Depression: America in the 1930s,* USA: Blackside.

Chris Whitely, *'Bebe Daniels'*, accessed 11/19. http://www.hollywoodsgoldenage.com/actors/bebe_daniels.html

Joshua Zeitz, *'Age of Convergence'*, accessed 11/19. https://ap.gilderlehrman.org/essays/roaring-twenties

Printed in Great Britain
by Amazon

43978183R00076